Marketing

Richard J. Watson

Chambers *Commerce Series*

Published by W & R Chambers Ltd Edinburgh, 1988

British Library Cataloguing in Publication Data
Watson, Richard
  Marketing.
  1. Business firms. Marketing
  I. Title
  658.8

ISBN 0-550-20714-7

Typeset by Bookworm Typesetting Ltd, Edinburgh

Printed in Great Britain by
Richard Clay Ltd, Bungay, Suffolk

Contents

Chapter 3 Pricing Policy

PART II PRACTICAL MARKETING

Chapter 4 Product Development

Chapter 5 Packaging the Product

Chapter 6 Distribution

Chapter 7 Sales Promotion and Merchandising

Chapter 8 Advertising

Chapter 9 Direct Marketing

Chapter 10 International Marketing

Chapter 11 Protecting the Consumer

Chapter 12 Franchising

PART III SALES AND SELLING METHODS

Chapter 13 The Sales Function

Chapter 14   The Basic Sales Skills

Acknowledgements

The examples and case studies throughout the text are drawn from practical experience gained throughout a twenty year career – from College Marketing Student to eventual College Marketing Lecturer – each move illuminated by well remembered names, faces and events.

My thanks are due to all those individuals and companies mentioned in the text, to staff and students at North East Worcestershire College for their contributions and practical comments, but mainly to my wife Peggy for the unfailing encouragement and support contained in each and every page.

Preface

Marketing abounds with specialised texts which investigate a particular aspect of our profession, but neglect the wider implications of marketing.

This text is written as an introduction to the central role of marketing in the heart of business operations, and to clarify this has been divided into three separate sections.

Section One introduces the theory and concept of marketing and its role in the company and the community.

Secondly, and most importantly, the text covers the practical aspects of marketing, enabling prospective marketeers to observe and practise marketing in action.

Thirdly, the text includes a comprehensive section on the skills of selling which, for many, represents the first introduction into the world of marketing.

R.J.W.

PART I

WHAT IS MARKETING?

Chapter 1

Introduction to Marketing

Marketing is an enjoyable and, above all, exciting profession, where theoretical application is joined with flair, ability and practical skills to form the foundation of every commercial enterprise.

For anyone wishing to enter the profession, the most effective way of gaining the necessary expertise is to make a conscientious effort to analyse, adapt and improve on the marketing being demonstrated in our daily life. Marketing affects the lives and living standards of every consumer throughout the world. We are exposed to the numerous facets of marketing every moment of our waking day. It shapes our needs, our desires, our working lives and our leisure pursuits.

We have all practised the skills of marketing to a lesser or greater extent, from a very early age. We may have been responsible for the designing of an advertisement to promote a school event, decided a suitable price at which to sell a second-hand motorcycle, or researched a suitable choice of holiday for a youth club membership. Marketing is not simply selling products or services. It is a combination of individual areas of expertise, designed to ensure that goods produced or services offered meet the needs of potential customers.

1.1 What is Marketing?

Let us begin by examining the official definition of marketing used by the Institute of Marketing:

> Marketing is the management process which identifies, anticipates, and supplies customer requirements efficiently and profitably.

As in all good definitions, the essentials are contained clearly and succinctly, and will form the basis of our further study of the subject.

Marketing is essentially a management process, requiring the application of a wide number of disciplines. It cannot therefore be carried out piecemeal, extracting only those areas which appear to suit a particular purpose. No organisation can expect to flourish by utilising advertising alone, or by choosing to simply sell.

To market we must identify the factors which will influence our customer, be it product design, delivery, or distribution. Having identified the factors, the management must anticipate the needs of the customer, and provide a product or service which meets those needs. Providing a product which meets the needs of the customer will be of little use if the product or service is not supplied in the form, or the place, in which the customer chooses to purchase.

Efficiency is the mainstay of all business management, but is of particular importance in marketing. Marketing cannot compensate for poor production or low quality goods, but in the present economic situation companies will still need to ensure that their marketing expenditure produces the anticipated results. Although marketing is not always conducted purely for profit, the requirement for a profitable operation cannot be over-stressed. Without an annual profit, companies will not be able to allocate capital fairly towards future marketing activities.

1.2   The Marketing Philosophy

If we examine organisations, we discover they have an essential philosophy in conducting their operations and dealing with customers. We could classify them in two ways – those that subscribe to a product philosophy, or those who believe in the sales philosophy.

Product-based

A product-based company or organisation may be seen by many marketing practitioners as the root cause of the decline in UK manufacturing. A company subscribing to this philosophy believes that provided it manufactures a quality product, efficiently and at an attractive price, the world will beat a path to its door. The results of this over-confident policy have been proven incorrect by the decline of manufacturing in the UK until it now represents only 20% of Gross National Product, compared with 30% of GNP during the early 1960s.

The flaw in this method of operating is the companies' failure to take account of the changes in customer needs. Whilst they continue to concentrate on reducing costs, or improving production, other companies with a marketing approach will provide the customer with the products they require.

Fig. 1.1 *Marketing Organisations*

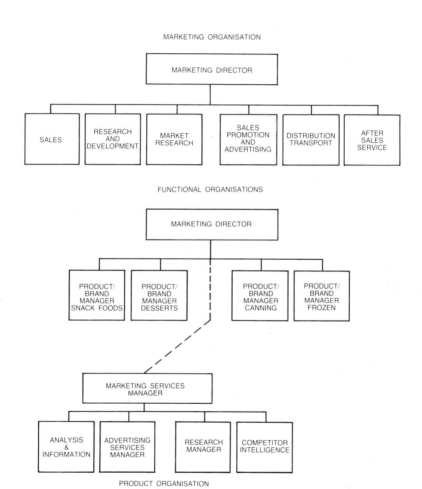

Example

The classic example of a product-based group of companies is the UK motorcycle industry. During the 1950s the British motorcycle industry concentrated on producing large numbers of a restricted machine range. By continuing with this product-based philosophy they ignored the developing demand for smaller, less expensive mopeds. This market opportunity was exploited by manufacturers from Japan, producing lightweight, cleaner machines to cater for the customer's demand for a simple method of transportation. From this initial point it was only a short step for the Japanese to expand into the differing segments of the market. Offering features such as electric starters, automatic transmission, and weather protection, which British makers had neglected to provide, it was but a short step to total domination of the market.

Sales-based

Organisations or companies who subscribe to the sales-based philosophy generate large numbers of orders through aggressive sales techniques, and thus become cost effective. This type of company concentrates on heavy expenditure in advertising, sales promotion and the training of highly skilled sales staff. By following this policy high turnover is generated, but the hidden flaw lies in the consequences of an unexpected downturn in sales.

The belief that customers are resistant to purchasing the products, or purchasing greater quantities, produces an organisation which concentrates on the techniques of persuasion at the expense of customer satisfaction.

While the results of this policy may at first provide spectacular results in increasing sales turnover, the policy is wholly dependent upon further customers joining the rush to purchase. Should there be a slight downturn in sales, the expenses of selling rise as a proportion of the sales generated. The costs of production remain the same, establishment expenses continue, sales staff still require salaries and commissions – the only budget that does not remain constant is the sales ratio. It is therefore easy to deduce that a rapid reduction in the amount of profit generated will be the ultimate outcome of this policy.

Example

For many years the market for domestic washing machines had been filled by several well-established manufacturers, until, in the early 1960s, a new name burst upon the scene. John Bloom, an entrepreneurial character, purchased a small company manufacturing electric razors, operating under the name of Rolls Razor. With financial backing he also moved into the importing of an inexpensive domestic washing machine. With this low initial cost and a high demand for this type of machine, sales were high. The Rolls washing machine became a fast-selling product. John Bloom moved into manufacturing within the UK. Through full-page advertisements in the national press, sales promotion and extensive free gifts, sales continued to increase. However, production could not keep pace with demand. Quality and delivery suffered, and customers became disenchanted with the product. With promotion costs at such a high level it was but a short time before the Rolls washing machine became uneconomic to produce, and the company moved quickly into insolvency.

1.3   The Marketing Mix

Having examined the two basic production and sales philosophies, we now realise that the role of marketing extends to the complete operation of the company. We must ensure that our marketing is responsible for the total concept. Marketing must cover the initial product conception, research, testing, pricing, promotion and distribution. This division of marketing and the amount of importance to be attached to each part, is known as the *marketing mix.*

For simplicity we refer to this mix as the four Ps of marketing:

> *P*roduct
> *P*rice
> *P*lace
> *P*romotion

Just as a cake recipe may vary in its ingredients to produce the correct flavour or richness, so the elements of marketing are combined to produce the most appropriate marketing mix. From the areas of marketing a company will select those which are appropriate to the product, to produce an individual marketing mix. We therefore need to examine the various factors which make up the 4 Ps of the marketing mix.

Product

- The required quality of the product.
- How long the product is expected to last.
- The chosen brand name for the product.
- How the product will be packaged.
- How many other products will exist alongside.
- What additional items can be offered.
- What after-sales service is expected or needed.
- What guarantees will be given.

Place

- By what method the product will be moved to the purchaser.
- How large an area will be covered by the distribution.
- What method of transport will be used.
- Where the sales outlets will be located.
- How the sales areas will be arranged.
- What level of stock will be required to meet customer purchases.
- Where warehouses will be located, if required.

Promotion

- What use will be made of advertising, face to face selling, publicity, public relations and sales promotion techniques.

Price

- What the basic price of the product will be.
- Will the product be offered at different prices in other markets?
- Will any discounts or allowances be given?
- What terms of payment or credit will be expected and offered.

The 'recipe' for the marketing mix will be decided by company management depending upon the results obtained from research, past experience of similar products in the market, business judgement and intuition. Each element of the marketing mix has an effect upon the others. An increase in the price of a product, without a resultant increase in quality, packaging, advertising or sales promotion would be a retrograde step in the mix.

Of considerable importance is the final image of the product in the mind's eye of the customer, and care must be taken to ensure that the new image does not conflict with existing patterns.

Rolls-Royce is internationally famous for the manufacture of a range of high quality motor vehicles. Their marketing mix takes account of the level of after-sales service required, the design of the vehicle, the price level, and the exclusivity of their dealerships. If the world-famous Rolls-Royce were suddenly to be discounted in price, advertised at 0% finance, and offered with free optional GT pack, would the marketing mix still be correct and what would be the effect of this change on sales of the vehicle?

Circumstances, however, may change within the market requiring an immediate alteration in the mix to retain the marketing impetus. The future development of new methods of retailing may require manufacturers to review price structures or increase the budgets for sales promotion techniques.

Fig. 1.2 *The production/marketing balance*

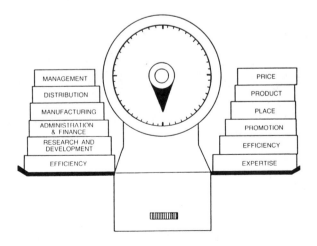

1.4   Definition of a Market

Throughout marketing we will come across several differing uses of the word *market*. In general terms it refers to a quantifiable area, sales value or category of purchases made by a specific type of purchaser. It may be used in conjunction with other definitions to give a clearer picture of the particular area we are trying to define. Use will be made of the term *consumer market* to define goods or services purchased by households. *Industrial market* will be used to classify goods or services purchased by manufacturers for use within their products or processes. *Retail market* will cover the purchases of a wide range of products through retail outlets.

These additional definitions, when attached to a market, will assist a company in deciding upon the methods of marketing. Each particular market has its own internal terminology, together with methods of assessing progress, techniques and promotion methods. Companies can well operate simultaneously within several markets, controlled by different staff, and operating often in isolation from each other, but offering identical *basic* products.

Example

Steriseal UK manufacture and market a range of pharmaceutical products used by hospitals, physicians and pharmacies. Each of the three separate markets requires wound dressings as a basic product, but marketed, packaged and priced in differing quantities, styles and methods. The hospital authority will require supplies in bulk, available directly from the manufacturer's stock, purchased under a yearly contract. Physicians will require smaller quantities, packaged with clear usage instructions, whilst pharmacies will wish to have supplies readily available from a local medical wholesaler. Each market has specific needs which could not be met by any one single marketing system.

1.5   Definition of a Product

As with markets, so products can be defined in a number of different ways. In the broad spectrum we may choose to split products into raw materials and finished consumer products.

At this stage it is wise to remind ourselves that for the purposes of marketing, a service should also be visualised as a product. A service retains the same attributes as a product, in that it can be advertised, distributed, researched and marketed. However, it remains intangible, and therefore requires constant attention to ensure the service continues to reach the standard the customer expects. We can classify the type of product being marketed under three headings:

Products from competing firms

Many products compete in the same market for a share of the purchaser's expenditure. These products will be similar to each other in general content or formulation, but offer real or perceived differences to appeal to a particular market segment. Let us consider the differing brands of tooth-paste. Each paste offers the same basic benefit of preventing tooth decay. Some will choose to offer fluoride as an addition, whilst others will count the removal of plaque as a consumer benefit. This brand personality exists with every product, and determines how the consumer visualises the benefits of the product.

Products competing in the same market

Companies compete within the same market for a share of consumer expenditure, although the products offered are radically different and produced by different processes. These type of products are known as substitute products. The purchase of product A will act as a substitute for the purchase of product B.

Example

Let us consider the market for edible hard fats. Some consumers will prefer the natural taste of butter, compared with the manufactured flavour of margarine. Each product competes against the others for a share of consumer expenditure. Each emphasises the differences between the products, often seeking to portray the other product as a less acceptable substitute.

We must carefully examine *all* other products which could compete for a share of our market, and not merely confine our marketing investigation to identical products from competing firms.

Different products competing for restricted expenditure

The purchase of an expensive product in one market may limit consumer spending power in another. These major purchases are a matter of an 'either/or' choice for the consumer. The choice may lie between the purchase of a family caravan or investment in a new kitchen. The purchase of either will lower the disposable income, and reduce the customer's ability to spend further within that period.

1.6   The First Steps in Marketing

Many of the international companies operating throughout the world came to prominence before the skills of marketing were fully understood or appreciated. From essentially small beginnings companies grew and prospered, based on the proposition expounded by Thomas Edison that if a person produced a better mousetrap the world would beat a path to his door.

When production became specialised and the population discovered that a comfortable living could be made solely from the manufacture of a single product, then the need for marketing arose. In those far-off days it was sufficient to nail a signboard to the door of the work place, giving the name of the craftsman and the product, with perhaps the addition of a distinctive symbol for the illiterate to comprehend.

The barber's red and white pole, the pawnbroker's sign and the chemist's flacon are past examples of the use of symbols to enable a business to be easily recognised.

In the modern world, with the international markets dominated by the use of all-media advertising, sophisticated distribution and product management, it is no longer sufficient to merely nail up a sign with your name. A small company must utilise the skills of marketing to the same extent as the largest international organisation.

Major companies invest considerable expenditure in the first element of marketing communication – the consideration of the correct marketing choice of:

- Company name
- Brand name
- Logo design

To protect this investment, names are registered throughout the world, with legal sanctions available against those attempting to trade or pass themselves off as another company. However, provisions in UK law control the use of names relating to royalty, or banking, or creating the impression of a larger operation than is the case.

Marketing has always resounded with instances of company and brand names which, while suited for the UK market, proved unacceptable in overseas markets. Colours, designs and understanding of names differ between cultures, the name or colour acceptable to one nationality striking an unhappy chord in others. For example, the influx of cars with names representing Japanese national pride or good luck signs – the Nissan Cherry-Blossom or Bluebird – relate more in the UK to shoe cleaner or caramel toffee than to the macho symbolism provided in the names of European cars.

1.7   Choice of Company Name

In addition to being a legal identity, the company name is a long-term investment around which we create a suitable image in the mind of the consumer. For the marketing practitioner the following basic rules should be given careful consideration when choosing a company name.

Personal

While the law makes no provision preventing us from using our own name, from a marketing point of view this is not always the wisest choice. An individual's name can become too closely identified with an organisation's successes and failures, causing problems if the business is taken over by larger organisations, or fails in a dramatic way.

Geographical

The use of a name attached to a particular geographical location restricts the area within which a business can market products. Consumers prefer to deal with organisations which are seen to be local, which is fine if your marketing plan envisages only local trade, but is of lesser use if adjacent markets are also your target.

Initials and acronyms

The tendency to shorten company names to initials or acronyms is a recent development in business. Research has proven that the consumer is less able to recognise the product range being offered if presented with a series of initials. In the UK we are all aware of the clothing retailer C & A. Less well-known is their original name of Continental and American Modes, dating back to the late 1920s. Only by extensive marketing and advertising can we build customer recognition of initials, the budget for which could be spent in more constructive areas.

Humour

Humorous company names are a double-edged weapon in marketing terms, ideal for catching the consumer's attention, but unlikely to develop further. Cleen and Prestwell Dry Cleaners may raise a smile, but will never become Cleen and Prestwell International.

Spelling

Correct spelling and ease of pronunciation of any company name prevents confusion when consumers seek information in the telephone directories, or other types of listing. Consumers are not prepared to spend time searching for Kristine's Kar Klean through each alphabetical listing.

1.8 Brand Names

Specially designed brand names identify individual products and enable companies to compete in differing market segments. Branding is an important part of the marketing strategy and allows suppliers to build customer loyalty to the product.

With brand names the marketing effort can be directed towards building around the product a definable image of quality, service, reliability, etc. Brand names may be the same as the company name, which in the case of well-known products allows marketing to build on the favourable image created, and eases the task of launching new products on the market.

A choice exists with companies as to the use of branding. Some retain the company name in the background, using brand names as the major promotion. Others use the company name on all products. We should always bear in mind that a problem with an individual product can, if it happens to be the name of the company, have a disastrous effect on the whole of the product range.

Example

A food canning company experienced a quality control problem with canned salmon, which received nationwide publicity in the media. The problem related only to one of the range of the company's food products, and other canned products were not affected. Consumers hearing of problems boycotted the total range of canned products bearing the name of the company, until the problem was overcome.

Certain rules also apply to the creation of brand names:

Series

If possible brand names should form part of a continuing series for in doing so they allow a cumulative effect to be built up. Consider a variety of names based on a single theme – precious stones, metals, etc. Mars confectionery utilise brand names based upon the parts of the Universe, i.e. Mars, Milky Way, Galaxy.

Individual

Any brand name should be individual to the product, and not merely an addition to an existing name. Adding *de-luxe* or *extra* to a name does not create another brand.

Sources

While many names are the result of brainstorming sessions between individuals, others originate from names within the company. The Winfield brand name came from founder Frederick Winfield of Woolworth, St Michael from Michael Seiff of Marks and Spencer, and the Delamere brand from the Tesco head office address. A useful source is to consult a copy of *Chambers Thesaurus* and pick names which have a bearing on the quality or image of the product.

Design

The brand name, style, colour or type used, if sufficiently distinctive in design, gives protection to the product by allowing it to be registered as a trade mark. Use of the name alone gives a small measure of protection, providing the company can show prior use, so registration is always advisable. A number of trade associations will keep a list of authorised brand names of their members, as an additional form of simple registration.

1.9 Logos

A logo is a distinctive badge or symbol which can be used instead of the full name, and yet continue to represent the company on promotional items or literature. When next watching a Grand Prix motor race or RAC rally, observe the number of logos and symbols which appear on the competing vehicles, a use which gains international recognition.

The opportunity should also be taken at this early stage to decide on a standard company colour scheme to be used as livery for the company vehicles, or to provide easy recognition of company premises. Motor manufacturers supply a comprehensive list of all standard colours available, so a selection can easily be made, with the additional advantage that the colour chosen is likely to be available for some considerable time.

For the sake of easy reproduction the logo should be designed as simply as possible. Too much fine detail is difficult to define when the logo is reduced in size, as on a company tie or badge. The logo should also be confined within a circle, square or some other regular shape, as only in this way can the logo be expanded equally in size. A logo should be capable of reproduction on the smallest or largest item belonging to the company.

Fig. 1.3 *Quota sales logo*

The use of carefully considered company names, brand names, logos and company colours is all part of the marketing effort designed to produce the correct image of the company in the mind of the consumer or buyer. A co-ordinated image builds confidence in both the consumer and in the company staff. Customers and staff feel that they belong, by their purchases, or by their efforts at work, to an organisation which displays a caring, quality or modern image in the marketplace.

Assignment

In co-operation with a partner you have decided to set up your own company offering a small range of specialised products. Your first task is to develop a suitable company name, utilising the basic rules stated in this chapter. Your range of *not more than* five products will each require an individual brand name, forming part of a series and capable of further expansion if required. You are required to produce a company logo giving an image of your company operations. Having completed these tasks you are to produce a correctly constructed letterheading based on the example shown below.

Fig. 1.4 *Example of letterheading*

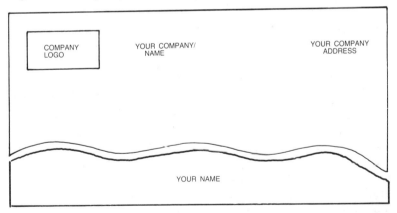

Your letterheading should be A4 size, utilising black dry transfer lettering, and capable of reproduction on photocopying machines. A sample package label should be produced using one of the brand names you have chosen, and showing the company logo.

Chapter 2

Marketing Research

In common with many areas of marketing, the role of marketing research is often misunderstood. There is a tendency to see only the public face of market research and to assume incorrectly that this represents the total.

Market research is merely one method of discovering information about markets, products, consumers, users and trends. Marketing research, however, examines five basic areas:

- Research into products;
- Research into prices;
- Research into sales promotion;
- Research into distribution;
- Research into markets.

The definition of marketing research offered by the British Institute of Management is:

> The objective gathering, recording, and analysing of all facts about problems relating to the transfer and sale of goods or services from producer to consumer or user.

Just as war intelligence is the hidden eye of the armed forces, enabling battles to be fought based on information of the enemy positions, so marketing research is the provision of quantifiable information which enables organisations to plan their marketing mix and strategy. We shall examine each area of marketing research in detail.

2.1 Research into Products

No company wishing to remain profitable will be so supremely confident as to leave its range of products unaltered for any period of time. Product research examines the product or service of the company, investigates the continued acceptance by the customer and the acceptability of the product design, usage and packaging. Product research undertakes test markets of products to determine the likely sales turnover if marketed nationally, in addition to comparative studies of competing products. From these test results, new products are developed, product ranges extended, or new markets discovered for existing products.

The history of business is scattered with companies who failed to take account of the changing requirements of their customers, failed to offer products revised to modern standards, and failed to note competitors' developments. To illustrate the motivation for continued product development, we need to examine a product's life-cycle.

2.2 Product Life-Cycle

We refer to the projected life of a product in terms of the life-cycle. Just as we have a life-cycle of indeterminate length from birth to death, and marked by periods of intense activity, so a product follows the same pattern. Figure 2.1 shows the product life-cycle of any product. The base line illustrating the time-span will vary with the type of product and the market in which it competes. Depending upon the type of product, this cycle could be as long as 20 years or as little as 20 months. Product research attempts to determine the stage a product has reached in the life-cycle by utilising data on sales, examining competitive developments, and sales projections.

At the *introduction* stage of a product, following its research and development, profits and sales can be expected to be low, for customers are slow to invest in an untried item, advertising will not have reached the total market, and prices may be high to recoup the heavy initial expenditure. During the *growth* stage, demand will grow for the product, resulting in sales at a high profit margin. For the moment the competition may have failed, or be unable, to react to this new product in the market. It may well be that steps have been taken by the company to protect the product, through patents or registered designs. However, it will not normally be long before the other companies develop a similar product to compete with the new entrant.

The product then moves to the stage of *maturity*. Sales increase more slowly than during the growth stage, the market may be moving towards saturation, and similar products move in to take a share of the market. The maturity stage is followed by a slow

Fig. 2.1 *Product Life-Cycle*

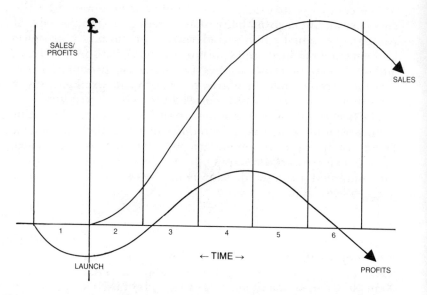

decline, if no new product supersedes, or a rapid decline if a new competing product offering improved benefits enters the market. During the decline, certain products could continue to provide a reasonable return on the low initial past investment, or be switched to a less demanding market, possibly, as in the example below, a market within another country.

Example

In the late 1930s the Volkswagen Beetle was designed by Dr Ferdinand Porsche as a people's car. The war interrupted his grand ambition to see every German worker driving his or her own motor. In 1947, under the control of the Allies, full manufacturing of the Beetle began. During the next forty years millions were exported throughout the world. When Volkswagen decided to introduce new designs, the production of the Beetle was transferred to Brazil, where production could be carried on at lesser labour costs. Production still continues, with a limited number of new Beetles being exported to Germany to meet the enthusiast's continued demand.

2.3   Market Research

There is a high probability that at some point we will be approached, usually in a public place, by a smiling interviewer carrying a clipboard and questionnaire. Questions are asked regarding our opinion on company advertising, or to discover our purchasing habits on a wide range of products. We are face to face with market research in action.

Market research is concerned with the collecting and collating of data which, when analysed, enables management to determine our attitudes, habits or buying behaviour. The major methods of market research are classified as:

1   External, or primary research
2   Internal, or secondary research.

Internal research can also be called desk research, while external is often referred to as field research.

2.4   Internal Research

This is the method of extracting statistical data from published sources. It has the advantage of being relatively quick and inexpensive but, not surprisingly, has the disadvantage of being not always relevant to the area being studied. The sources which can be used are many and varied, and considerable ingenuity is required to discover the particular source where the appropriate statistical information may be found.

Her Majesty's Stationery Office is the source for most governmental statistics, including trade performance, the national census, and indexes concerning the economy. Local government may be able to provide restricted statistical information on population spread, unemployment, etc. Trade associations and trade magazines, such as the *Grocer*, are often a fruitful source, together with inter-company performance comparisons collected for certain major industries.

The alert marketeer will not neglect information available within his or her own company, by taking the opportunity to collate statistical data contained within customer records, invoices, purchase records, or from the annual accounts and publicity material of competitors. The sales force is a useful source of market research intelligence, often providing high quality information. The provision of pre-printed cards detailing the source and data obtained, for return to the marketing department, will ensure that valuable information is not ignored.

All published statistics are, by their very nature, out of date and give only an indication of market trends. Desk research is useful in the initial stages of product development, or investigation into possible trends. If the data is to form the basis of important marketing decisions, then field research should be considered as a final and conclusive check.

2.5   Field Research

However effective desk research has proven, at some stage in the market research process consideration will have to be given to the use of field research. In general terms we must first ask the question: 'Will the information obtained by carrying out field research affect the decision to launch a new product?' Should the product have reached such a stage of development that the data obtained would have no influence on the marketing plan, then field research should not be used merely to confirm existing prejudices.

The method to be used will depend on the importance of the information required to make the marketing decision, and the ease, or difficulty, of obtaining the specific data. Field research may be undertaken by:

(a) questionnaires mailed to participants;
(b) telephone interviews;
(c) group discussions;
(d) panels convened to 'blind test' products;
(e) face to face interviews;
(f) behavioural observation;
(g) hall test.

Questionnaires mailed to participants

The advantage of lower research costs when using post questionnaires is offset by the reduced response rates from the sample population. Provided the questionnaire used is short, the method produces a faster response over a wide sample.

Care must be taken to reassure respondents that the results of the sample will remain confidential, and that the data provided will not be utilised by sales departments to undertake unwanted sales calls. True anonymity over respondent names must be maintained. Some less than ethical surveys attempt to discover names from hidden codes or keys within the questionnaire.

A postal questionnaire will enable respondents to consider the answers carefully, or to check on the accuracy of data before replying. However, there is a strong possibility the questionnaire may be biased by being read carelessly and answered in total, rather than as individual replies.

Telephone interviews

The use of telephone samples allows for improved anonymity and speed. Respondents do not feel as inhibited as with personal interviews, being prepared to answer provided the questions are kept short. Questionnaires can probe in depth, and allow any misunderstandings to be eliminated. Telephone interviews are quick to carry out, reach the point speedily, and are well accepted by respondents. Popular in the USA, but used to a lesser extent in the UK, the telephone interview is a simple way to conduct accurate market research.

Group discussions

A preselected group of respondents are called together to discuss, under the control of a researcher, a chosen subject or to solicit opinions. The researcher seeks to control the interview and discussion without imposing his or her opinion. This method is usually used to discover an opinion on consumer products by allowing discussion to flow over design, suitability for purpose, or product acceptability. The results will be tape recorded for later analysis. Group discussions allow 'in-depth' or 'deep-rooted' prejudices to surface, and alterations or improvements to presentation or product to be quickly arranged.

Panels convened to 'blind test' products

A spread of suitable consumers are recruited to undertake long-term testing of a product range. These tests are conducted blind, in the sense that no indication is given as to origination, brand or manufacturer. The reports produced from this are collated over a lengthy period, often testing different products, packing and formulation. By altering just one element of the product formulation, for example by changing the speckles in a washing powder from blue to green while retaining the previous package, washing characteristics and perfume, it is possible to determine the customer response to each element of the product.

By continuing to test one characteristic against another, research and development hope to arrive at the most acceptable product for a cross-section of the public. Difficulties arise through the natural tendency of consumers to express average opinions, not wishing to 'upset' the provider of what are essentially free samples. Blind testing by using panels therefore requires considerable expertise in framing the questions to determine the real opinions, and considerable care to ensure that details of any new products under test do not reach the attention of the competition.

Face to face interviews

Although the most expensive method of conducting market research is by face to face interviews, the advantages outweigh the ultimate cost. During personal interviews the chosen questions can be altered to suit the circumstances, or misunderstandings eliminated before the response is given. To reduce costs a smaller sample is often used, causing concern for the statistical accuracy of the results obtained.

True market researchers will be members of the Market Research Society, and will carry suitable identification. An increasing misuse of market research by companies seeking new clients under the guise of a questionnaire-type survey is to be condemned.

Field research by personal interview investigates attitudes, habits, or the behaviour of the consumer. The most visible use of market research is during the UK General Election, when results are published almost nightly during the campaign.

As in the case of product testing, the use of direct questions does not always reflect the true feelings, opinions or habits of the interviewee. All too often the answers reflect what the consumer thinks they should do, but not what they actually do. As an example, a question asking 'How often do you use the bath or shower?' will not always result in a true response – most interviewees giving a figure well above the proven actual usage. These deeply hidden motivations or behavioural patterns can only be fully understood by the use of actual observation.

Example

In order to discover the number of electors likely to vote for a particular party during a general election, it is not necessary to canvass every voter leaving the polling station. Instead, a number of parliamentary constituencies are selected where voter characteristics accurately reflect the national average.

A simple questionnaire requesting the voting choice likely to be made will result in a number of answers expressing the opinion of the electorate. These results, if extrapolated for the whole country, can be expected to reproduce the voting trends of the total voting population. The questioning of a single sample of only 1,250 voters during the last election accurately reflected the actual voting pattern of over 14.5 million voters.

Behavioural observation

With direct questions the result is direct answers, which therefore fail to highlight the hidden desires, emotions or intentions of the customers. This new form of market research seeks to discover the underlying reactions of consumers by simple observation of behaviour. Observation of customers within a retail outlet would quickly highlight the behavioural aspects of shoppers, giving immediate information on the time taken to make the purchase decision, movement patterns, or the most effective positioning.

When combined with in-depth interviews and the use of projection techniques, where consumers are asked to place themselves in an imaginary situation and give interpretations of their feelings and reactions, this method can produce worthwhile insights into human behaviour patterns.

Hall test

Products are displayed in a suitable hall or public venue, and members of the public are shown a selection of products available. With the aid of question techniques, opinions are sought as to the suitability of the products displayed, and which product features are seen as most acceptable.

2.6 Undertaking Market Research

Field research relies on the questioning of a sample of the general population, and the processing of those answers to give a result which could be applied to the population as a whole. These results are usually expressed as a percentage figure that statistically reflects the opinion of the whole.

The sampling frame

The design of a suitable sampling frame is the initial stage of any field research process, and determines which type of person or organisation are to be questioned during the survey, and where or when those respondents may be found. If we wish to question a selection of teenagers it would be necessary to draw our sample from places where teenagers may be expected to gather – dance halls, discos, cafés or youth clubs. If a more accurate sample is required it may be necessary to define the sample population further by age, sex or social grouping in order to ensure the sample frame reflects accurately the distribution throughout the population.

2.7   Social Grades

At this stage it is as well to examine the use of social grading which occurs time and time again throughout all marketing. By classifying our population into differing social grades, we are able immediately to quantify the characteristics inherent in each group. From social grading we can discover people's tastes, habits, patterns of buying, and indeed their whole way of life. With the universal use of social grading, manufacturers can determine which of their products appeal to a particular group of customers and, for example, ensure that they are then advertised in the newspaper which has the highest readership amongst that group.

The essential quality of social grading is that it should permit long-term comparison from survey to survey over a period of years. An analysis of the population by groups will vary less over a period of time if these groups are classified by occupation rather than by income limits, which are subject to constant change from pay awards. The use of social grades is therefore now based purely on occupation and, unlike the old system, does not reflect the background of the person concerned. The use of terminology such as upper class, middle class and lower class, with the connotations of breeding, caused considerable resentment in those so labelled.

Grading is by the occupation of the chief wage earner and not by the titular head of the household, as this more accurately reflects the social and economic status of the household.

Fig. 2.2 *Social Grades in the United Kingdom*

New grade	Old grade	Occupation	Population percentage
A	Upper middle class	Top social/business leaders	3%
B	Middle class	Senior executives, managers	11%
C1	Lower middle class	White collar office workers	18%
C2	Skilled workers	Factory workers	34%
D	Semi-skilled, unskilled working class	Manual workers	28%
E	Lowest level of subsistence	Students, pensioners, unemployed	6%

Grade A

Informants from Grade A households represent about 3-4% of the population and will usually be a professional person, own/operate a successful business, a senior civil servant, or have considerable private means. Examples include commercial airline pilots, Church dignitaries, established doctors or dentists, local government senior officers, heads of public schools or large secondary schools, stockbrokers and large land-owning farmers.

Grade B

Eleven per cent of households represent the middle class and occupy less prominent positions in industry and the professions. Examples include college lecturers, supermarket managers, vicars, senior managers in industry, senior bank clerks, senior journalists.

Grade C1

Eighteen per cent of households are made up of families of small tradespeople and non-manual workers carrying out administrative, supervisory and general clerical jobs. Examples include curates, insurance agents, parks superintendents, librarians, clerks, typists, technical grade engineers, police sergeants, RN sub-lieutenants.

Grade C2

This group represents 34% of households, consisting in the main of skilled manual workers and their families. When doubts arise between skilled and unskilled working class, it may be possible to check by asking the respondent if they have served an apprenticeship, although not all skilled workers have this qualification. Examples include factory foremen (over 14 employees), charge hands, bricklayers, plasterers, painters, coal-miners, welders, ambulance drivers, shop assistants with responsibility, post office sorters, HGV drivers.

Grade D

This group consists entirely of manual workers, generally semi-skilled or unskilled, and accounts for 28% of households. Examples include bus conductors, railway porters, gardeners, clothing machinists, dough mixers, traffic wardens, caretakers, army privates, meter readers.

Grade E.

This group consists of old age pensioners, widows and their families, casual workers, and those dependent upon social security schemes through sickness and unemployment. They constitute 6% of the population.

2.8   Choosing the Sample

The total number of consumers or companies from which we take our sample selection is known by market research as the *universe* or *population*. From this we will select a certain number of people to question, which we refer to as the *sample*.

Random sampling

There are a number of differing ways of conducting a survey, the most unbiased being based upon a random selection from the population. The selection of persons to question by random methods ensures that the problem of distortion or bias does not affect the results of the survey. Bias refers to the strong possibility that the results could be distorted by the sample being taken from identical sections of the population, and not from the wider universe. For example, if, when conducting a survey into the shopping habits within a town centre, questions were asked only at one particular time of day, the answers given would not accurately reflect the habits of the total population. Questions would have to be asked at random times throughout the day in order to discover the true picture.

In a similar fashion, should questions on the consumption of beer be asked only of those of the public leaving a public house, the results would be biased in favour of high consumption, and not reflect the normal pattern throughout the population. To ensure a true selection we can use a computer to generate a series of completely random numbers, in much the same manner as the computer used for choosing the winners of Premium Bonds.

Fig. 2.3 *Example of Computer Generated Random Numbers*

20	12	42	156	256	409	283	839	278	209	348
3	39	58	20	199	37	387	189	799	328	187
12	66	238	189	398	29	32	233	198	237	336
13	33	20	23	238	459	495	39	478	210	598
129	448	228	549	227	38	28	23	444	228	399
84	328	299	218	736	18	3	28	48	275	

These can then be used to select names from a directory, membership rota or mailing list. This method is usually used in governmental surveys, taking name from the list of electors or similar national lists, where the characteristics of the population are unimportant to the information needed. The index of retail prices is calculated in this fashion, by choosing names at random from the electoral register and requesting that all purchases made over a period of time are recorded. In this way a cross-section of the population is used to discover the typical purchase pattern of the nation.

The cost of conducting a random sample in this way is considerably greater than most other methods, as specific names are chosen who then have to be interviewed. Allowing for the number of people who may not be available at the time the interviewer chooses to call (requiring a considerable number of 'call backs') the total cost can be up to three times greater than other types of survey.

A purely random choice of person to question reduces the bias which may occur with the interviewer choosing. It is only natural that an interviewer will select an apparently pleasant individual to interview, rather than one who from their appearance appears to be 'anti' interviews. However, this problem of interviewer bias does not occur with a random list, as there is no choice of whom to interview, merely a list of names and addresses to contact.

Interval or probability sample

A variation on the full random sample is to use the interval or probability sample where names are selected from lists at regular intervals, say every tenth name, which brings a certain element of randomness to the survey. Researchers use the notation 'n' as the interval chosen – nth sample.

Quota sampling

To effect cost reductions over random sampling, marketing will use the quota sampling method where the interviewer is instructed to find quotas, or numbers, of the required category of person.

The quotas are in the proportions of the total numbers occurring under each particular quality required. This could be the simple proportional split between male and female in the population, requiring the interview of approximately 52 men to every 48 women. To this could be added the quota for age of population, smokers, or non-smokers, wine drinkers or non-wine drinkers, employed or unemployed, until we reach the situation where we are seeking to interview six 20-25-year-old males, who smoke, drink wine, and are unemployed, and five 30-35-year-old females who neither drink nor smoke, and are employed.

Despite this difficulty it is the task of the interviewer to discover suitable persons for interview during the preliminary questions. This, in itself, can lead to bias or error on the part of the interviewer through laxity or over-anxiety to obtain the correct respondent. They are often willing to accept an interview with a person who does not completely match requirements.

2.9   Designing a Questionnaire

This is never an easy task, but it is still attempted by many amateur marketeers, often with a significant failure to obtain useful information or statistics. It is not sufficient merely to list a series of questions in an attempt to extract information from a respondent. The questions themselves can be insufficient, ambiguous or biased.

Insufficient questions impart only simple information or an opinion, where the answers are dichotomous, being restricted to a mere Yes, No, or Don't Know. We have all had experience of this type of question and the results obtained, mainly through the use of this type of survey during elections. If we have the major expense of a market research survey, then we must obtain the maximum information possible during the time available to us.

Ambiguous questions are the most common mistake in many surveys. The question is constructed badly, and the answer, while appearing to give the correct information, fails to reveal the total picture. As an example, if we wish to discover the number of households using video cassette recorders, and we ask people the question, 'Do you own a video cassette recorder?', their answer may well be no. The use of the term 'own' implies legal ownership, but the person may well have a VCR in the household subject to a rental or hire purchase agreement. Far better to ask, 'Do you have the use of a video cassette recorder?'

Questions must always be carefully phrased to ensure we are gaining the correct information. To check this we either carry out a test run of our questionnaire with a very small sample, observing any areas which cause ambiguity, or leave the construction of the questionnaire to the specialist market research organisation, who employ psychologists to examine the hidden meanings within a questionnaire.

Bias or distortion can occur in the phrasing of the question, usually in the use of a leading question. While the words used may be leading – 'Don't you think the Government have made the economy worse?' – the method of asking the question must also be taken into account. The interviewer must not express opinions by the use of visual or verbal signals – a raised eyebrow or a smile. Neutrality in all areas is the key to questioning techniques. Interviewers must be well-trained to ensure that their own opinions do not obtrude.

Bear in mind the desire within the public to give the 'right' answer to a question. Questions which may reflect badly on the habits or opinions of a person will not be answered freely, for fear of producing an adverse reaction from the interviewer.

Assignment

The traders in your local shopping centre wish you to conduct a survey amongst the shoppers using or visiting the centre. Your task is to conduct the survey, using market research methods, to discover:

- Location of customers;
- Traffic flow;
- Reasons for using centre;
- Opinions on the centre;
- Improvements or alterations to the centre;
- Any additional information you consider important in discovering the consumers' opinions of the centre.

You are to gain the permission of all those in authority involved in the centre before commencing the survey. On no account is the survey to be conducted other than in a public place. Some form of personal identification will be required as authority to conduct the survey. Your results will be presented in the form of a report which will collate the information obtained during your survey, together with a summary of the information in the form of a graphic presentation – bar charts, pie charts, etc.

Chapter 3

Pricing Policy

The vital area of any business is in the correct pricing of the product being offered to the consumer, firstly to ensure an equitable profit to the company, and secondly to encourage the consumer to purchase the product. When setting out to price a product or service, it is wise to remember that:

Turnover is vanity – Profit is sanity.

High turnover will create extra demands on production, finance and distribution, and often cause the company marketing system to break down. Far more sensible a path is to consider carefully the pricing structure of your product, to ensure that turnover grows, but still returns a profit to the company.

There are four basic types of pricing theory:

3.1 The Market Price

From the earliest age we develop and practise our skills in deciding what is a fair market price for any type of good. Market price can be seen by the consumer as a 'fair' price for a commodity, a price which is similar to the competition, or a price they expect to have to pay.

Cast your mind back to childhood and the inbuilt understanding of the exchange rate required for those school playground bartering sessions, with the rate determined by demand and supply. The complex negotiations over exchanging stamp collections, the swopping of comics, and the loan of bicycles. What negotiations did you undertake to decide a fair price? Was it based upon the amount of the product available, or

33

the difficulty of obtaining supplies? If a product or item was in short supply, did not the price rise accordingly?

We accept that the price of salad tomatoes should rise in the winter when extra freight charges are incurred in flying them over five hundred miles from the Canary Islands. But we also expect the price to fall when the summer produces a glut of UK tomatoes. That is the law of market price. Put simply – if the price of a product rises to such an extent that consumers are put off purchasing because of price, then demand will fall. The price then drops because of lower demand. Then up goes the demand because they are now less expensive, and the whole cycle starts again.

A market price is in certain cases set by a formal market system, where products are offered and purchased both for present consumption and for the future. An example of this formal market structure is the operation of the London Metal Exchange, where buyers invest in the 'future' market for a variety of metals based on the anticipated demand.

By charging less than the market price, the result is not to stimulate demand, but to produce an impression in the mind of the customer that the produce is in some way defective or of lower quality. A higher-than-market price produces an impression of overcharging, unless apparent benefits are included in the cost, such as higher quality, faster service or improved credit terms. Products which are structured on market price prove to be those where the demand is directly related to supply, a drop in price, or an increase in the production or availability, will increase the demand.

However, the theoretical approach of the economist is not always the case in practice, assuming as it does that demand will increase if the price is lowered. The reduction in price can often only improve the demand by a marginal amount, as consumers do not have an automatic desire to increase consumption. Reduction in the market price will often result in an alternative purchase being made with the income released.

The market price structure is exemplified by the Organisation of Petroleum-Exporting Countries (OPEC), who attempt by negotiation to set a market price for crude oil exports. These attempts are often undermined by the failure of producing countries to keep to agreed production restrictions. The flow of oil increases, resulting in the market price being lowered to compensate for overproduction in excess of demand. The consumer may well increase the use of petroleum, making more journeys for pleasure reasons, although this will have only a marginal effect.

3.2 The Psychological Price Barrier

The price of a product is in part determined by the appeal it makes to a person's sense of value. It is quite possible for a product to be seen as too cheap, or equally well as too expensive. This feeling is not always related to the perceived or actual value, but rather to the image generated by the product. A combination of these factors can be seen in an attempt by the then Austin of England Motor Company to launch an addition to their range of executive motor vehicles with the introduction of an Austin saloon powered by a Rolls-Royce engine, and thus to be known as the Westminster RR.

The combination of the prestige name, attached to an essentially mass-produced vehicle, conflicted with almost all the psychological price barriers. Consumers who desired the prestige of the Rolls-Royce name were unhappy with the use of the Austin marque for a premier priced vehicle. Those consumers who wished to enjoy the benefits of luxury executive transport at a reasonable cost were unhappy with the premium price being asked for the use of a Rolls-Royce engine, but without the additional status luxuries normally included. Simply put, consumers who wanted a Rolls-Royce thought the Westminster RR too cheap, while those wanting an Austin found the car too expensive.

Determining the price to take account of psychological barriers requires considerable investigation, which could be carried out by the use of a hall test (see Chapter 2).

Psychological pricing also refers to the method of displaying prices, used mostly in the motor trade, where the cost of a car at £4999 is apparently considerably less than £5000.

3.3 Economic Price

This is a price which represents the actual cost of manufacture, plus overheads, and a fair profit margin, compared with the price being asked within the market. If, after determining these factors, the product could not be sold at an economic price, then there is no point whatsoever in seeking to launch it on the market.

3.4 Discretionary Pricing

Having taken from the income of a household those essential expenses such as rent, mortgage, living costs, etc., we are left with a certain amount of discretionary income which we could spend on luxuries. It is up to the discretion of the household as to how they would wish to allocate the amount available. Companies operating in this type of market are conscious of the demands of alternative luxuries, and will thus find themselves competing with products carrying the same luxury tag. Marketeers should be aware of this type of pricing structure and continue to check, not only on competitors in their market sector, but on other luxury-segment products.

3.5   Penetration Pricing

The decision may be made to set the price of a product at a very competitive level, often by accepting a lower profit margin than usual. By reducing the margin, the manufacturer or supplier hopes to penetrate the market and grab an increased sales volume. Actually they 'corner' a larger share of the market and can eliminate any competitors, who will soon realise that a limited or reduced share is unprofitable and leave the market.

This method of pricing can usually only be undertaken if the market and product are seen as having a long life-cycle. If the product is subject to the vagaries of fashion, or has only a limited sales potential, then penetration pricing is a reckless policy to pursue. Penetration pricing relies on gaining a large share of the market and thus firmly establishing the brand in the mind of the consumer.

3.6   Skim Pricing

Every manufacturer aims to make such an initial impact on the market with a new product that the competition is caught by surprise and is unable to offer a similar advantage.

Should a company be involved in a market segment known for its short product life-cycle, then they charge a high price to skim the market while sales are buoyant. The consumers may complain at the apparently high prices charged for certain products, but at the same time be willing to pay the price because of their needs. If a product should prove popular and achieve a high market share while protected by patents or registered designs, then skim pricing is almost always to be expected.

By using skim pricing we are seeking to remove the 'cream' from the market by setting a high initial price. This is carried out in order to recover the heavy initial investment costs incurred by the research and development department.

Example

A recent example of skim pricing was the policy alteration within the UK Health Service, whereby medical practitioners were banned from prescribing branded drugs if an unbranded standard product was readily available at lower cost. The drug manufacturers raised a considerable outcry, pointing out that the high profit margins on branded drugs were intended to recover the considerable sums expended on development and research. These investment costs are recovered through the use of a skim pricing policy before a competing drug enters the market, or a new development makes the drug obsolete.

As shown above, government regulatory bodies and market pressures can investigate suppliers' pricing policies, and if these are proved unreasonable in the circumstances, can force down prices even if a monopoly situation appears to exist. In this case skim pricing becomes an unreasonable policy to retain and causes damage to the image of the supplier in the eye of the consumer.

3.7 Price Lining

When a company has marketed a range of branded products in a single market segment, the prices of individual items could be set on a scale which progresses from low price-low quality through to high price-high quality. This relationship is known as price lining, where the individual product prices are both related and separated.

As an example, we would look at the price lining structure for a motor vehicle manufacturer. At the bottom of the range of vehicles would be the standard two-door hatchback with a small capacity engine, standard fittings and little luxury. Priced a little higher would be the luxury two-door hatchback, with a larger engine capacity, carpet, fitted radio cassette, and special trim. In the middle of the range would be the standard four-door traditional saloon, with a larger engine but little luxury. Top of the range would be the luxury four-door executive saloon, with every conceivable fitting and luxury.

Should prices increase at the bottom of the range, then in order to preserve the relationship and the differential structure, prices may have to increase throughout. We could have the situation arise where the middle of the range four-door saloon becomes so close in price to the four-door executive saloon that buyers are prepared to 'trade up' and sales of the middle range will suffer.

Price lining is a useful policy in keeping a grip on a market, but it does need considerable control when used, in order to prevent price differentials being blurred in the mind of the buyer.

3.8   Single Price Policy

A single price policy could almost be referred to as the 'best average price policy' where a supplier sets a price to give an adequate return whatever the quantity of product sold, wherever the product is sold, and to whoever the product is sold.

An example of a single price policy is in the supply of utilities to the domestic market, where gas and electricity are priced according to units consumed – with no discounts for increased quantity, or reductions for being closer to power-stations or the North Sea!

3.9   Negotiable Prices

A price is set, based on costs of production and required profit margins, but is then subject to negotiation with buyers. Should a buyer be able to take larger quantities, or arrange for cost savings on deliveries by introducing palletised loads or mechanical handling, then the price will vary.

WARNING – ensure that the negotiating ability of large buyers does not obscure the need to continue to make a profit. When introducing a new product on to the market, do not be tempted to negotiate lower prices as a means of entry, but rather look towards a short-term sales promotion (Chapter 7) as more likely to achieve a better result.

3.10   Loss Leaders

Less used than was formerly the case, loss leaders are intended to encourage the consumer to buy a product priced at less than cost, in the hope that this purchase will encourage the buying of higher priced or more profitable items at the same time.

3.11   Contribution

Pricing is partly the responsibility of the marketing department, together with production and finance. Many of the problems which arise in setting a suitable price structure are caused by marketing practitioners who are often untrained in finance and costings, and therefore unable to understand many of the essential areas of formulating a price.

While this section is not intended to offer a full financial insight, it is wise for marketing executives to understand the general principles of costing, fixed overheads, variable overheads, semi-variable overheads and contributions made by products. Let us examine briefly the factors which go to make up a price costing exercise.

Fixed overheads

Every business from the largest international to the small sole trader has fixed expenses or overheads, which are incurred whether the business achieves low or high sales.

Example

Fixed overheads can be seen when we examine the role of British Rail in loss-making services on branch lines kept operating as a social service. When BR run a mid-morning train service from a small market town to a major conurbation at only 50% of full capacity, they will lose money; let us say this sum could be £5000. If this service was withdrawn we would discover that BR would now lose £6000. The reason is of course that the fixed overheads are still being incurred – the wages for signal staff, track maintenance staff, ticket office staff, drivers, guards, porters, etc. The reduction in fixed overheads when a train runs is solely due to the contribution of £1000 made by passenger fares collected on the journey.

Fixed overheads by their nature can only rarely be reduced significantly if a company cut the scale of operations, by taking smaller premises or making staff redundant.

Variable overheads

These are costs incurred during the manufacture or distribution of a product which will vary in proportion to the number of items manufactured. Usually applied to raw materials, labour costs, services or utilities, they can be reduced by improved efficiency or through negotiation with suppliers.

Semi-variable overheads

Costs which increase slightly in line with production or capacity, but do not exceed a maximum overhead. For example, to introduce a night shift at a factory will increase the expenditure on lighting costs, but this figure can only rise to a sum equal to the total hours of darkness. The amount of product manufactured has no influence on the amount of lighting consumed.

Marginal costing

When pricing products or services we need to examine all areas of operating and overheads to see if we can produce savings by increasing output. On some occasions spare capacity is available within an organisation to undertake additional work or manufacturing. The marketing department should consider whether to take on a product which gives little profit, but whose sales turnover will make a contribution to reducing the overheads.

The idea of marginal costing is that once the overheads, both fixed and variable, have been covered by the past sales, all future sales represent an extra profit to the company, even though the profit be small. This is often called the break-even point, and once again the marketeer must be aware of what is meant by the break-even point, and apply this to his or her own products.

Example

The question is often asked why a ticket for a scheduled flight between Birmingham International Airport and Schipol Airport Amsterdam is sold at a far higher price than is available through tour operators. The costing of air flights depends upon the percentage loading. Each passenger represents a contribution to the operating costs, fuel, airport landing charges, etc. Any seat not filled reduces that contribution. In a scheduled flight the aircraft must depart on time be it fully loaded or merely with one passenger. The higher cost of scheduled flights represents the element of risk in running the aircraft on a regular schedule basis.

3.12 Pricing and Profitability Exercise

The marketing target/sales form (Figure 3.1) combines in a single exercise many of the overheads and costings required by those setting up a new company or marketing operation. It forms a useful exercise for those students of marketing who wish to utilise a single document to discover if a business proposition is viable, and is recommended as a suitable target sheet for any existing businesses.

The importance of a target for marketing a business cannot be overestimated. It is not sufficient merely to hope to make a profit, or hope to control expenses. By completing the target sheet a marketing executive will be able to:

1 decide an accurate target for sales turnover during a set period of time;
2 decide if a proposed operation is viable and will be capable of meeting profit or turnover targets;
3 decide if an existing business or operation is suitable for purchase or takeover;
4 judge the success of an operation and make management or marketing decisions, based on facts and figures.

Do not falsify figures in carrying out this exercise. An overestimate of expected costs will produce a higher target for required sales turnover, but even this is a wiser course than underestimating. In general terms expect to receive ten orders, be prepared to actually get five, but make sure your business is viable on only three orders.

You can decide to target yourself for a weekly, monthly, half-yearly or yearly turnover figure. The difference lies in the accuracy of the target. With a yearly target the problem lies in the long period which elapses between the setting of one target and the next. Sales can drop badly over such a long time, making corrective action more difficult. Shorter targets allow for seasonal variations, and marketing alterations can be made more quickly.

To obtain the required figures for each section, we can use our experience with previous businesses, or examine similar types of company operations in the market. Should you be considering purchasing an existing business, then request of the vendor a set of the previous accounts, together with copies of all recent bills, invoices or projections. Information on typical rentals, rates, insurances, salaries, etc. if not available from the vendor, or existing records, can be obtained by interviewing local business executives, or by visiting your local authorities for average figures.

Let us take each section of the target form and examine in detail how the figures may be found and calculated. Each figure is numbered, and should be entered in the appropriate square opposite.

Example

A1 SALARIES/WAGES   *24,000*

Section A

General overheads also known as *fixed overheads*

Any business or marketing operation will incur expenses before one single solitary product is sold to a customer. These expenses are known as overheads, and represent the cost of operating the 'background' parts of a company.

A1 Salaries and wages
Let us begin by deciding the amount of salaries and wages you expect to have to pay for all full- and part-time staff involved in administration, non-selling or production areas. An example of this type of staff would be secretaries, receptionists, caretakers, manager/ess, etc. For instance:

Example

Two part-time secretaries	£8000 pa
One full-time manager	£12000 pa
One part-time security guard	£4000 pa
	Total £24 000 pa

Target figure for Year £24 000; month £2000; week £480

A2 Rent
Calculate the rent or lease which will be paid during the target period.

A3 Rates
Record general and water rates for target period.

A4 Insurance

Calculate the cost of all business insurances. Examples include fire, consequential loss, public liability. Do not include vehicle insurance in this figure.

A5 Depreciation
The initial cost of plant or equipment, divided by your estimate of the useful years of life, will give an approximate figure for depreciation. For example:

Example
> Equipment value: £2000
> Years of life: 10
> Depreciation of approx. £200 as a target figure.

A6 Repairs
A nominal figure will usually be sufficient for expected repairs to property or equipment. Vehicle repairs and services are not to be included.

A7 Heat/light/power
Calculate a total figure for all utilities incurred in the business from copies of past accounts or previous bills.

A8 Telephone
Take into account all expenses for the provision of a business telephone, including rental and call charges.

A9 Postage
Postage charges incurred in the control of the business, but not charges involved in sales promotion, direct mail, etc.

A10 Stationery
A large amount of stationery will be required for the new business venture – examples include letterheading, envelopes, invoices, etc., but do not include stationery or print used for sales promotion activities.

A11 Bad debts

Take into account an amount set aside for any debts from customers who prove unable to pay – to be classed as a business expense in the same way as any other.

A12 Discounts

Any amount given to customers paying by monthly credit terms is known as settlement discount and is normally set at 2.5% of the goods total. It is classed as a business expense.

A13 Legal charges

Take into account any charges incurred in setting up the company, obtaining leases, or involved in the granting of licences or other legal matters. Usually higher during the initial setting up of the company.

A14 Accountancy fees

All companies will incur charges for the preparation and auditing of the company annual accounts.

A15 Sundries

Estimate any fees, licences, training courses, donations, etc.

Total the individual amounts shown under each category from A1 – A15 and write the figure in the space for Section A total. This then forms the target for the general overheads or fixed expenses which the business or marketing operation must meet.

Section B

Capital employed

In any business proposition the marketeer must ensure that a sufficient return is made on the amounts invested. The return on capital employed is a figure which is often forgotten by most small businesses when commencing to trade. The capital amount could be invested in a far more secure investment, without being exposed to any of the risks involved in a new marketing or business venture. If we do decide to invest in a new business then we must be sure that we may expect a reasonable return on capital employed, in addition to any payment for our duties as proprietor or director. To carry this out we need to enter the value of our various capital items under the headings shown, and then to calculate the total value.

B16 Land
Should your business venture require the purchase of land, then the value of that holding should be entered. Bear in mind that the value of the land can rise.

B17 Buildings
Enter the value of your investment in purchasing buildings. Once again remember the value can rise, and the current value should always be shown. The purchase price of the land or buildings when the original investment was made must be subsequently adjusted in line with current values.

B18 Equipment
Enter total value of investment in plant and fittings.

B19 Vehicles
Enter initial costs of any business vehicles, whether new or used.

B20 Value of stock
The major part of any business investment is in the amount of the company stock holding. An average stock value figure should be used for this entry, calculated from an actual recent stock check.

B21 Credit to customers
All businesses may have to extend some form of credit to customers, although all businesses should avoid this wherever possible. Take an instant check on any actual amount, or expected amount, of credit extended to customers at any single time.

B22 Cash in hand
Some marketing operations do require a certain amount of capital to be kept in the form of cash. Any investment in this liquid form should be entered in this section.

B23 Goodwill
Only an existing business venture can have an investment of goodwill. Goodwill represents the value attached to the good

name of a company, and is represented by the amount by which the purchase price exceeds the value of the capital items shown on the balance sheet. We can calculate the amount of goodwill paid, or required, by totalling the value of headings B16 – B20 and subtracting this sum from the total price. For example:

Example
Total value of B16 – B20 for *Quota Sales*

Land	£12 000
Buildings	£23 000
Equipment	£7000
Vehicles	£5000
Total	£47 000

If Quota Sales Ltd is being offered for sale at £67 300 then the goodwill element is valued at:

Sale price	£67 000
Capital investment	£47 000
Goodwill ∴	£20 000

To decide if the value attached to the goodwill element in a company is too high or low, then it is normal to multiply the audited net profit of the business by a factor of 3.

Net profit each year	£10 000
multiplied by 3 =	£30 000
Goodwill	£20 000

It can be seen that the goodwill element of the price being asked is reasonable.

B24 Other investment in business
Certain types of business operations require additional investments – possibly licence or franchise fees. These should be included under this heading as an investment in the business.

B25 Credit from suppliers
Any amounts allowed by suppliers to the business in the form of

credit could be said to represent a capital investment. Take the average amount of credit given to the business by suppliers and enter under this heading, which is then deducted from the total of capital invested.

Add the total of amounts under headings B16 – B24. Then subtract the total of B25. This figure represents the total amount of capital invested in the business. If this sum were loaned to the business by a clearing bank, the current loan rate of interest would be charged. If the capital invested has come from private sources then an equal return should be expected, as compensation for the loss of interest.

Example

Total B16 – B25	£110 000
Less B25	£10 000
Total therefore	£100 000
Current bank rate	18%
Return should be 18% of £100 000, or £18 000 pa	

Section C

This section is for the expenses incurred only when *operating* your business. If you have several sections to your operation – retail, wholesale, manufacturing, service, repairs, etc. – then complete a section for each area. It could be that certain staff duties are spread amongst the various departments, and in this case allocate the expenses for these staff by time or turnover.

C26 Salaries and wages
Enter a figure for wages paid to full- and part-time staff employed in sales or production-type occupations.

C27 Cleaning expenses
Enter figure for wages paid to full- or part-time staff, and cleaning materials.

C28 Sales promotion and advertising
Enter the actual or proposed amount to be expended on these activities.

C29 *Vehicle expenses*
Enter the running costs of company vehicles, servicing, taxation, repairs and insurances.

C30 *Commissions and bonus payments*
Enter amounts paid to sales representatives or staff as an addition to wages.

C31 *Sundries*
Enter any extra expenses incurred.

C32 *Consumables*
Enter the cost of any items used in operating the department.

Add the total of amounts under headings C26 – C32.

Section D

D33 *Proprietor's salary*
This is a salary to be paid to the owner or owners equivalent to the salary paid for similar duties by an employer. The salary of a manager/ess would be included in heading A1.
Transfer all totals of Sections A, B, C, D and total.

This figure represents the minimum profit contribution which the business must produce.
   This profit will come solely from sales of products. Taking the average profit margin on the individual or range of products, we can then determine the required sales target. This can be seen in the following example:

Average profit margin	33%
Required minimum profit contribution	£10 000
Therefore, minimum sales turnover must be	£30 000

If the projected sales turnover needed to achieve the required profit contribution is seen as being greater than the capacity of the market in the initial stages, then attention will have to be given to reducing costs. Expenses for using a company vehicle could be reduced by leasing, as could the investment made in office equipment. We could also ensure that telephone, heating, lighting and other utility costs are reduced, and that all staff costs are carefully considered. Decisions may have to be made as to whether part-time employees would be more suitable than full-time, or even if staff are really required for certain types of duty.

The advantages of this control-form are the ease with which alterations can be made to many of the aspects making up the marketing plan, and the speed of discerning the effect these have on the required sales target. The sales-target form can easily be transferred to a spreadsheet program and calculations updated automatically.

Assignment

Having been unemployed for a considerable time Frank Page decides to develop his hobby of tropical fish breeding into a full-time business venture. He decides to call his retail outlet Tidewater Aquarists, and sets about finding suitable premises in his local area. After a lengthy search, he manages to obtain the lease to 46 Highcastle Street, at an annual rental of £6000 pa. His general rates and water rates will cost him £2000 pa and he manages to negotiate the necessary insurances for £400 pa. Heating and lighting requirements will be slightly greater than the previous tenant's, as he needs to operate a number of heaters and pumps, but he estimates a total figure for this of £1000 pa.

Frank expects the cost of telephone calls and rental not to exceed £180 for the year, and the postage to be around £50. His legal charges are more than he expected, due to his solicitor having to negotiate and then double-check the lease, but he is quite happy with the estimated costs of £120. His accountants have agreed to charge a nominal fee of £100 for his first year's trading and audit. He does not intend to employ any staff to keep his accounts and administration under control, but intends to carry this out himself.

The equipment he intends to use is mostly second-hand, but some comes from his hobby collection. He values it all at approximately £3000 and expects it to last for five years before it needs replacing. For the moment he decides not to invest in a vehicle, but to concentrate his money on purchasing stocks of tropical fish, food, fish tanks and a wide range of accessories. He reckons he would need to invest around £6000 in his stock. However he would be allowed credit, with companies who have agreed to supply him, of around £500.

He decides to employ his daughter Caroline as a part-time sales assistant every Saturday, and expects to pay her around £500 per year. Keeping his stock of tropical fish in top condition, Frank expects will cost him at least £200 per year in food and equipment. Frank decides to advertise in the local free paper when he opens, and to have 2000 promotional leaflets printed.

These he expects to cost around £500. The consumable items Frank uses, including his essential supply of tea bags, milk and sugar, together with carriers, bags, etc. should not exceed £200 per year. Finally he decides that with a little car he and his wife could manage on a salary of £10 000 pa.

Frank intends to work on a profit margin of 50% on all his stock. Your task to therefore to calculate his REQUIRED SALES TURNOVER using the sales target form (Fig. 3.1).

Fig. 3.1 *The Marketing Target/Sales Form*

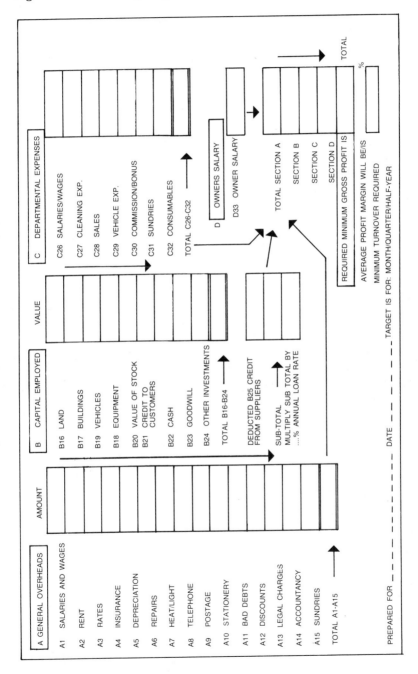

PART II

PRACTICAL MARKETING

Chapter 4

Product Development

If a marketing executive were to be questioned on which single marketing procedure presented the greatest risk factor in the investment of time and capital, without doubt the answer would be 'the development and launching of a new product'.

Each week in the UK grocery market alone over 100 new products are launched, of which only three may have a chance of real success. However, before we conclude that a new product has almost no possibility of success, it is worth recalling that a single successful product in this market can produce sales income in excess of several million pounds.

4.1 Discovering New Product Ideas

Very few individuals or companies are blessed with the ability to suddenly discover a completely new product concept. The period of time taken to develop many popular products from original concept to marketable version is to be numbered in years rather than months.

Example

Video	6 years	1950 – 1956
Ball point pen	7 years	1938 – 1945
Instant coffee	22 years	1934 – 1956
Helicopter	37 years	1904 – 1941
Television	63 years	1884 – 1947

While the product idea may have been invented some considerable time before the launch, the difficulty lies in transferring the new technology into a form which is acceptable to the market.

Marketing abounds with cases of product concepts taken to manufacturers and rejected out of hand as having 'no demand at present'. In equal measure, cases still occur of manufacturers being so convinced of the concept that they fail to consider what demand is being met, and whether the new product manages to meet those needs.

Example

Sir Clive Sinclair provided the concept of the small electric-powered vehicle in the Sinclair C5 which, although meeting the need for an economical form of transport, failed to satisfy the consumer need for comfort, prestige and safety.

4.2   Sources of New Product Ideas

Companies often have a considerable amount of expertise in an area of production or design which often provides the base for the development of new products. Few originate from a conscious attempt to develop new products, but more from the adaptation of an existing viable item to suit a new market.

The company sales force also form a useful source of new product ideas and suggestions, and are encouraged to report instances of customers requesting new items or seeking alterations to the present range which could then be offered to a wider market. The internal workforce of a company, involved in daily production and design, can, through the simple expedient of a suggestion box, produce additions to the range. Approaches are also made to companies by inventors seeking a market for the results of their enterprise.

Not all inventors are so successful. In order to avoid any product idea being neglected or ignored, the most effective practice is to analyse all suggestions or approaches through a set of fixed procedures.

4.3   New Product Development Sequence

Each product must pass through a minimum seven-stage evaluation process designed to delete non-viable ideas before being launched on the market. This process will consist of:

1 initial screening process;
2 first financial feasibility study;
3 capital requirement analysis;
4 business forecast and cash flow;
5 technical development;
6 market research;
7 test marketing.

Initial screening of the product

In a similar fashion to vendor rating, undertaken by buyers before agreeing to deal with suppliers, so a new product is assessed under the contribution the product will make to the company and the customer. By giving a weighting to the required characteristics, the proposed product can be assessed to ensure it meets the minimum factors needed to succeed. If below this level it can be removed with little or no initial cost. On average almost 20% of new products will fail at this first stage.

Products will be rated by the company marketing department under the following headings:

(i)   fills a proven customer need;
(ii)   within present manufacturing capacity;
(iii) utilisation of existing resources and abilities;
(iv)   capable of continued profit contribution;
(v)   compatible with present product image/range.

The total rating score is the determining factor in a product progressing to the next stage. An idea may score high on the 'proven need' category but low on the 'utilisation of existing resources' by requiring a considerable investment in new plant and machinery. By using this method we avoid the 'favourite child' syndrome, where an executive, having been involved too closely in the initial evaluation, pushes a product through the various stages, despite evidence that it would fail to qualify when assessed under the five-factor scale above. Product scores under each of the factors will need to be re-evaluated again and again throughout the screening process.

First financial feasibility study

This is an investigation of the feasibility of all the factors involved in producing or manufacturing the product. Financial factors are evaluated, including the return on capital employed, and by checking against stated profitability targets, the group seek to discover which product gives the most effective return to the company.

Capital requirement analysis

Availability of capital, whether from external or internal funding sources, can be a major factor in the decision to manufacture a new product. New plant and machinery can be purchased outright, or subcontracted. Leasing of equipment can assist where the financial contribution is heavy, by using income generated to provide funding.

Business forecast and cash flow analysis

Consideration is then given to the income/sales turnover expected from the new product. Based on the projections supplied by the marketing department, the likely sales during the first two to three years of the introduction are determined as accurately as possible, by plotting a variety of circumstances. This will be calculated as a 'worst possible' projection and a further 'best possible' figure to give a high and low figure.

Technical development

Based very much on previous experience, gained while introducing new products, this evaluation will involve the production department of the company in calculating any technical difficulties, time-scales, production problems, replanning, workforce alterations, etc. involved in the project.

Market research

By this stage the product has been thoroughly evaluated within the confines of the company, and the moment has arrived for a more extensive evaluation by means of possible external market research. Suitable market research methods for the investigation of customer reaction to the product concept are detailed in Chapter 2.

4.4   Test Marketing

By using the process of test marketing we hope to reduce the risks and expense involved in launching a new product on the market. A test market enables the product to be launched in miniature in a smaller geographical area with market data being collected from the resulting sales. Test marketing is the moment when all the preparations – the market research studies, product design, product mix, market segmentation, and marketing plans – combine to produce a sample launch enabling us to check that all will run as expected on the actual day.

The first difficulty is to determine the area in which to carry out the test marketing of the new product. To be able to draw viable conclusions from the test market data, the prime requirement is to test in an area which carries the same target population and market segments as the national average.

Many of the advertising media, in particular the independent television regions, often promote the areas being covered by their network as being ideal test markets for products. Naturally, they are seeking to maximise their advertising revenue, and it would be foolish to imagine that a test market in miniature can ever be fully representative of a national market. The area which causes false assumptions to be made from the results of test markets is the expectation that a test market will remain standard throughout the period of the test.

When any marketing promotion or advertising takes place during the period of a test, the result is to increase the total level of activity in the market place. This activity alone tends to produce false indications of the likely product acceptance by the consumer or buyer, and therefore alters the potential sales turnover of a new product. A test market is the moment when a product 'goes public' for the first time, and naturally allows any competition clear access to the new product, the product formulation, design, promotional mix, test advertising, and indeed the sales figures obtained by the testing company.

In the world of marketing skulduggery, it is common for a competitor to learn of the test market exercise through the alertness of their sales force, and to immediately put in hand a comprehensive defence promotion.

Example

A snack-food supplier learns that their major competitor in this sector is test marketing a new potato-based snack in the Grampian Television region. Instructions are sent immediately to the sales representatives operating in the area to offer a 5% discount on all purchases to every retail outlet.

With stocks of snack products being promoted in store displays, the retailers are not prepared to invest in the product being test marketed. Consumers are encouraged to stay loyal to the existing brand, and to purchase larger amounts of it because of the discount being offered. The new snack receives a lukewarm reception from retailers and consumers as a result of this 'spoiling'-type promotion activity, and the snack is withdrawn from sale having failed to achieve expected targets.

Market expansion

Increased activity in a test market, or indeed in any market, results generally in an expansion of the total market.

Example

In marketing the Bovril stock cube, intended to compete against the long-established Oxo, the resulting marketing activity resulted not in the reduction of Oxo's market share, as may have been expected with a new competitor, but rather in an expansion of the total market share by some 18% for both cubes. Customers responded to the increased activity by purchasing more of both brands.

Test market data collection

Data should be collected carefully on the test market, as the natural tendency is to bias statistical data in favour of the product. Often figures are collected showing initial high 'sell in' sales, but no evidence is given on the 'sell out' figures. Products test marketed could be still in stock somewhere in the chain of distribution (Fig. 6.1), and the figures produced merely reflect an excellent initial selling job – not a continued and constant sales turnover.

Future of test markets

Many companies now find test markets produce figures which can be more easily obtained through product and marketing testing, resulting in the importance of test marketing being reduced to the level of a study to ensure the product has a potential for success.

4.5 Reasons for Product Failure

The main reasons for a product failing to achieve the correct level of sales, when launched, are generally due to a combination of the following factors.

(a) *Analysis of the product idea proves to have been poor.* The initial product idea did not have sufficient appeal to fill a gap in the market, or the gap did not exist.

(b) *Production budget undercosted.* The costing of any product idea is always difficult, but efforts should be made to ensure that the worse possible combination of circumstances is used as the base line, rather than the most favourable.

(c) *Competitive activity in the market.* Many products are launched on the market as a pale imitation of an existing product. When sales drop following the activity of the launch period, those products offering few added benefits are the first to disappear under the pressure of competition.

(d) *Change in the demand for the product.* Products launched on the market at the end of the life-cycle will find themselves in a secondary position to new products offering improved benefits and features.

(e) *Poor market research.* Poor analysis of market research findings tending to favour the launch of a product, caused by the self-interest of those executives involved in development.

(f) *Poor analysis of the test market results.* Bear in mind that the increased sales and marketing activity during the test market can give a false impression of the product potential, which fails to materialise when the activity ceases.

(g) *Launch dates mistimed.* There are a variety of reasons for the launch being mistimed. It is often due to a combination of circumstances outside the control of the company. However, if press attention and advertising are required, the dates of the launch should be kept as flexible as possible.

(h) *Poor promotional effort.* During the launch period the activity was not co-ordinated to give the maximum impact in the market place. If a launch is undertaken piecemeal, with marketing activities such as sales promotion, point-of-sale display, advertising, exhibitions, press releases and publicity being carried out in isolation, then the impact is missing, and the bandwagon effect fails to materalise.

(i) *Conflict between production and marketing departments.* Time and time again in the UK certain products fail to achieve continued high sales turnover due, not to a failure in the marketing mix or strategy but as a result of the production department of the company being unable to match demand. With marketing providing the demand, if production cannot keep pace, the normal course of events is that the demand will be satisfied by a competitor.

With one or two exceptions, the reasons for failure in a product launch are laid firmly at the door of marketing. The reluctance on the part of marketing executives to drop a product at any of the preparatory stages, when the research shows it is unlikely to succeed, is one of the major reasons for unjustifiable expenditure on poor launches.

Chapter 5

Packaging the Product

A common factor to all marketing is that products have a period of popularity, then disappear from the market, to return later packaged and presented in a slightly different form. Developments in the present packing of products show clearly the way that the package has evolved into an integral part of the product.

One hundred years ago our Victorian forefathers developed methods of printing full-colour reproductions on a variety of surfaces. Alert businessmen suddenly realised the huge potential in promoting their products on the actual container. Mass marketing demanded mass packaging, and the sheer physical effort of hand weighing, filling and sealing of products hampered developments.

With tin-plate containers, manufacturers had a means to promote the contents, increase the resistance to damage, and the ability to use machinery in improving the speed of packaging. Before this date the normal methods of packaging consisted of wooden crates, paper bags, sacks or plain glass bottles, often marked simply with details of the contents and the maker.

Since then we have seen the evolution of cellophane, metal foils, plastics, polystyrene foam and one-trip glass bottles, each offering a new method of promoting, protecting and advertising the product. New developments offered easier access and protection for the contents; clear plastic gave increased visibility and display, while improved sealing methods allowed easier dispensing. Nevertheless, in recent years consumers have begun to turn against the additional cost of over-packaging and the damage caused to the environment by careless disposal. Recent developments show a return to the early principles of bulk buying and plain packs marked simply with the details of contents and the maker. Thus the cycle is almost completed in one hundred years.

5.1   Design

Package design is a specialised area related closely to marketing, carried out by professional designers skilled in the development of new packing methods. They discuss jointly with the research and development department the marketing requirements of any new package, to determine the most effective materials, design and methods to achieve success with the ultimate consumer.

As consumers we expect our products to be packaged in certain ways, and remain naturally resistant to any sudden changes. Traditional packages become fixed in the mind of the consumer, and any alterations need to be carried out gradually over a period of time. Normally the proposed new package should conform to the essentials of good package design outlined in the following pages.

Individuality

(a) Has the product package sufficient individuality to separate it from other similar competing products?

Each product must have an individual identity, which will separate it from others in the same market. The customer will expect the product to be easily recognisable in order to quickly select the product they require. This can be based on colour, pack style or size. Certain manufacturers consider these packs so important to their marketing that designs are registered as trade marks. Lea and Perrins Worcester Sauce is packaged in a traditional glass bottle whose design and shape is known throughout the world. Despite other makers offering almost identical sauces, Lea and Perrins' bottle remains the product we expect to see behind every cocktail bar. Haig Dimple Whisky follows the same pattern, of a bottle design so unusual and important that it has become part of the brand name.

(b) Does the package form part of the same family of designs used with other products from the company range?

Retaining the family resemblance is important. It allows the brand to gain strength from repeat purchases. Having once purchased a product the consumer will automatically transfer the benefits perceived in one product, across to the new. This can only happen provided there is a strong family resemblance between products. It can be observed in the similarity of typestyle, colour and general appearance of all the products from the Nabisco range of cereals and biscuits.

(c) Does the package carry the same identifying logos, typestyles and company colours as the rest of the range?

To retain continuity between packages we use identical colours, typestyles and logo. Harrods of London carefully specify the particular shade of green used on all packages bearing their name, together with the special typestyle used wherever their name is repeated.

Convenience

(a) Does the product package have an in-built advantage, by having an after-use?

Almost any product can be packaged within a container that will allow after-use. With the vast number of polythene containers available ex-stock from suppliers, even the smallest companies can pack their product in a strong reusable container which can then be merchandised with removable labels.

(b) Is the product packaged in the correct size for use by the consumer?

As packaging developed, so manufacturers found themselves unable to continue offering single items. To recoup the additional costs of the extra packing, goods had to be offered in multiple packs. The consumer does not always wish to purchase in these greater quantities and marketing research should be undertaken with the pack to ensure that the quantity is acceptable. Examination of the market segment and usage quantities will enable the forward-looking marketeer to ensure the product is supplied in the correct size.

Manufacturers of dry batteries seem to have an uncanny ability to package their product in quantities which force the consumer to purchase at least two batteries more than are needed to power the radio!

(c) Can the package be used in small quantities by the consumer, or will opening destroy the potential for future storage?

The ability to reseal a package containing items of a perishable nature is essential. Consumers dislike waste, especially with items where the quantity used requires lengthy storage. Frozen foods in particular should be so packed as to allow removal of sufficient food for one meal, and to be returned resealed to the freezer. Examine each product to discover if it meets this criterion.

(d) Is the product convenient for storage, before sale, by distributors and retailers?

We need to look carefully at the external packing of products when supplied in wholesale quantities. Packaging has a selling function, while packing is mainly concerned with information and protection. The simple corrugated cardboard carton remains the most popular choice in providing protection, and carrying information on the quantity, size and contents.

Increasing use is made of shrink-wrapping and labelling, where the bulk product is arranged on a suitable base, ranging from a wooden pallet to a simple card, and then completely covered with special film, which is shrunk to fit by the application of warm air. This method has the advantage of allowing the product to be seen through the film, preventing delivery frauds and highlighting damaged products. In the case of cash and carry warehouses this method aids brand recognition by the visiting retailer, and forms an attractive bulk display.

The common building brick once transported in open vehicles, and often merely dumped on site, is now shrink-wrapped, secured by plastic straps and palletised to allow mechanical handling. The result is better protection and, more importantly, less broken bricks.

Transportability

(a) Is the product package easy to transport between locations?

Mechanical handling using fork-lift trucks has revolutionised all transportation throughout the world. We have almost reached the stage where traditional containers are a rarity, and some may regret the demise of many associated crafts. No longer does the local cooper hand-make a barrel. Modern beer drinkers expect the preconditioned aluminium cask. Wicker containers for fish, fruit and vegetables were superseded by wooden crates, which are now being forced out by moulded polystyrene packs. While the package may offer cost reductions by being handled in larger quantities, we must bear in mind that not all consumers or markets have the facilities to handle these heavy or bulky packs. Export markets in third world countries may be unable to undertake mechanical handling, relying instead on simple manpower.

(b) Is the package sufficiently robust to resist damage from transportation?

An often forgotten aspect of packages is the amount of rough handling sustained in even the simplest method of distribution. Water, dust, heat and security must all be considered before entrusting the product to the tender mercies of the carrier. The objective of packaging is to ensure the product arrives in the hands of the consumer in the same pristine condition as when it left the supplier. A test package should be sent through the chosen distribution system, and checked carefully on arrival at the destination, to ensure the packaging will resist the elements.

(c) Does the package reduce weight, size or storage needs?

The marketing department ensures that the latest developments in packaging technology are examined to see if savings can be made in weight, size or the need for storage. Modern materials and production methods allow products to be transported and stored in less critical conditions. Freeze-dried products, sachets, high strength plastics and design of packs produce worthwhile savings.

In the past, few carbonated-drinks producers had the ability to gain a national market, and generally restricted themselves to supplying local needs. Carbonated drinks in wooden crates had a high transport cost, through their tremendous weight. Modern shrink-wrapped plastic bottles allow reductions in transport costs and lower prices at the retail outlet, resulting in brands being available throughout the country.

Advertising and display

(a) Does the product package reproduce well in advertising?

A strong package design will reproduce with more effect in whatever medium is chosen. If the design is too complicated, the consumer will not easily recognise the product when on display. Strong design includes the shape of the product, the boldness of the brand name, the overall impression and, finally, the colour choices.

Colours used in packaging tend to follow certain set patterns expected by the consumer. Some of these preferences are natural – we expect milk and cream to be packaged in white containers. But others are contrived by the manufacturer (instant coffee tends to favour dark reds, browns and greens). While colours are often related to particular cultures, they do not necessarily automatically transfer to foreign markets. For example, in Iran the colour of mourning is blue, in Japan white, while in Latin America the funereal colour is purple. All of which shows the need for comprehensive investigation into the suitability of a package before transferring to a foreign market.

(b) Does the package stand out well in single quantities, and in mass displays?

A good package will be able to stand out when displayed as a single item, yet retain the same attributes when displayed in mass. The stacking ability of a package is one of the important areas to consider in overall design. Display space is always at a premium in any retail outlet, and stockists will prefer a product which can be displayed in as many ways as possible. Packages which cannot be merchandised on the shelf because of their awkward shape will not gain full sales benefit from the allocated space.

(c) Does the package match others in the range and conform to corporate image?

British Airways recently expended several million pounds on revising the corporate image of its aircraft, vehicles, tickets and staff. Although a Boeing 747 is not your simple product package, it does signify the importance the company attaches to the retention of a co-ordinated image throughout the company.

The product package is often the only physical contact between a manufacturer and the customer. Consumers develop a feel and a liking for a particular style and type of package. Manufacturers change the package very much at their own risk, aware that changes made are likely to be rejected by the consumer. Should a new product be marketed under the company banner, then consumers will relate it to others in the range, comparing it favourably or unfavourably. Packaging can give an impression of quality, and the marketeer must confirm that any new product launch retains that impression with the consumer.

Legal requirements and safety

(a) Does the product package give clear instructions for use?

The package is not only a protective covering for the product which helps to sell and display, but it is the medium for imparting information on the product and how it is to be used. The manufacturer has a responsibility to inform the user of the potential hazards, correct dosage or cooking methods.

With the wide spread of different ethnic groups within the UK many have difficulty in reading English, so the manufacturer should consider the use of pictures to express warnings or instructions. Illustrated in this form we can prevent customer disappointment, or even injury, and stop subsequent complaints or adverse publicity.

Products intended for export require even more careful instructions, as many countries do not understand either metric or imperial quantities. The advice of agents within the country should be sought, to discover the normal method of measurement used by the consumer. Instructing the population of Burma to add two tablespoons of milk to a cake mix is a pointless exercise, although some would say the same problem would be found in the UK!

(b) Does the package conform to all regulations concerning contents, quantity and ingredients?

An absolute minefield of regulations, recommendations and legal requirements exists to trap the marketeer. With the increasing power of the consumer, and a greater awareness of potential hazards of products, government and the EEC add new regulations daily to the existing lengthy list. Contents must be expressed in metric and imperial, ingredients shown in descending order, additives must be shown by EEC code number, and country of origin shown. Contact with the Department of Trade, chambers of commerce or trade associations will enable advice to be sought over labelling in accordance with present regulations.

(c) Is it safe against careless handling, and does it protect the consumer?

The regulations covering labelling are extended into the area of safety. The regrettable part is that many new regulations are introduced only as a consequence of a tragedy, often involving young children. The normal domestic kitchen has more dangerous products contained within its walls than the average factory, but few attempts are made to reduce the accident rate. Marketeers must concentrate on making any hazardous products 'idiot-proof' by taking steps to prevent accidental injury from misuse. Research carried out in the casualty departments of UK hospitals shows that opening a tin of corned beef is the single most common cause of severe injury to the finger!

Examples

The use of blister packs, where the product is contained within a plastic dome attached to a display card, allows manufacturers of hand tools the opportunity to improve the sales display, give detailed instructions on use, and prevent shop theft.

Garden insecticides are now frequently packaged in specially constructed containers, which allow only the correct dosage to be dispensed. Marketing can then offer the consumer the major benefit of safety in use.

The major movement made by the wine trade into 'wine boxes' instead of the traditional glass bottle increased the quantity of wine sold in a single purchase, without an increase in the cost of packaging, while retaining the ability to keep the contents in peak condition.

5.2 Package Development

Part of the development of a package design should include the use of a 'stand-out' test, where a number of designs are made up and the consumer is then asked to decide which product has most appeal – or 'stands out'. A well-packaged product will encourage extra sales. Many areas of marketing rely extensively on the packaging of a product to make the initial sale, either by giving a prestigious appearance, or enhancing the gift appeal of the product. Almost any product can benefit from improved packaging, and one of the major criticisms levelled against UK manufacturers is their lack of expertise in this area.

Assignment

1 Using an existing product package of your choice, design a new and more effective way of packaging the product offering as many of the following benefits as possible:

Ease of use
Protection and safety
Convenience of use
After-use
Improved visibility of display

2 Your task is to design and execute the exterior artwork on the card package illustrated in figure 5.1. You are to choose the contents of the package from the following list of suggested products:

1 Crème perfume
2 Frozen prawn cocktail
3 Sun-tanning crème
4 Beef drink
5 Custard cream biscuits
6 Engine oil treatment
7 Stain remover
8 Shoe polish
9 Surgical bandage
10 Pottery container with lid.

The package is intended to merchandise the product through

retail outlets, and must therefore be both attractive and informative to the consumer. Restrictions of the printing process to reduce costs mean that only three colours can be used in designing the package artwork.

The package should carry as a minimum the following information:

1   Product name and description
2   Promotional copy
3   Instructions for use
4   Information on size/weight/contents
5   Supplier's name and address
6   Bar-coding

The illustration in Figure 5.1 can be copied on to suitable card using the 5 cm scale grid. When the design of the package has been completed, the case can be simply constructed by cutting around the solid black lines, folding inward along all dotted lines and sealing tab A to position B.

Fig. 5.1 *Sample Packaging*

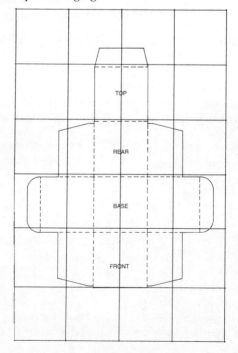

Chapter 6

Distribution

Distribution is of major importance to marketing, for without good distribution not one product would reach the consumer.

The distribution system in the UK has been built up over the past two hundred years. The Industrial Revolution, powered by steam, fuelled by coal and forged from iron, produced large quantities of goods – far more than could be absorbed in the local market. Those manufacturers who invested in building canals did not do so for the sake of improving the fishing, or to take a canal holiday. They saw the canals as the smoothest, fastest way of moving heavy goods to the major areas of population. The Duke of Bridgewater wished to move coal from his mines to the market, so he funded the first canal in England. He repaid his investment from the extra profits made by supplying quality coal in the place it was most needed.

Canals gave way to railways and the speed of distribution improved. The population moved to areas served by rail, confident that products would be available where they wished to buy them. Once a village developed into a city the population depended upon the efficient distribution of goods from all parts of the country. The expectations of the population grew apace with the improved methods of distribution, and the markets expanded.

Distribution is now so developed we accept without question that our local supermarket should stock fresh avocado pears from Israel, lettuce from California and prawns from Malaysia, giving little thought to the international chain of distribution which has brought this about.

6.1 The Rights of Distribution

To understand and remember the purpose of distribution we use the four rights of distribution:

- The right product
  in
- The right place
  at
- The right time
  in
- The right quantity.

Needless to say, if we follow this sequence then we are enjoying the benefits of an efficient distribution system, to fully back up our marketing efforts.

6.2   The Distribution Chain

Just as an anchor chain relies on the strength of the individual links, so the chain of distribution is composed of individual links between the manufacturer and the consumer, anchoring both together. Figure 6.1 shows a typical chain of distribution for manufactured, agricultural and imported products, and the path taken to move the goods into the hands of the ultimate consumer.

Fig. 6.1 *Simplified Distribution Chain*

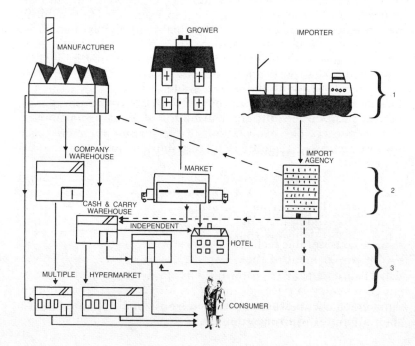

In Stage 1, manufacturers prefer to sell their products in bulk, to a limited number of customers. They have neither the organisation, nor the time, to supply a vast number of small accounts with limited amounts of goods. Manufacturers' prices are based on a continuous flow of large orders, from wholesalers appointed to cover a certain market area. In this way the orders received from their retail outlets are effectively bulked together for transmission to the manufacturer.

Stage 2 illustrates the different types of wholesaler, breaking down the bulk orders received from the manufacturers into the right quantities for purchase by a retail outlet. Wholesalers can be of the traditional type, breaking bulk orders into saleable quantities, delivering the required orders to retailers and offering credit facilities. More common is the cash and carry wholesaler, who again breaks down the bulk supplies from the manufacturer but offers neither delivery nor credit. Smaller retailers visit these cash and carry warehouses, which are usually situated on trading estates close to large conurbations, select cases of items required to replenish stocks, pay for their purchases and transport the goods themselves. In return for the retailer undertaking this effort the prices charged by cash and carry wholesalers are usually less than from a traditional wholesaler. Admittance to these cash and carry wholesalers is restricted to genuine retailers, and the public are not allowed to purchase.

Larger multiple retail outlets like Sainsbury, Tesco and Gateway operate a central purchasing system operating through their own wholesale distribution depot, supplying goods from manufacturers only to their own outlets.

Stage 3 illustrates the final movement of products through the various retail outlets into the hands of the ultimate consumer.

6.3 Choice of Distribution System

In general terms the shorter the distribution chain, the lower the ultimate price to the consumer. In marketing any product the decision has to be made as to which method to use.

Manufacturers or importers of specialised products which require considerable technical/sales expertise, will be best served by the employment of their own direct sales force. In this way they ensure that buyers receive the required level of installation and after-sales service, despite the higher costs and limited number of clients who can be dealt with. Products of a more general appeal will require wider distribution, and in this case the choice must be to move the products through the wholesale distribution system.

Wholesalers will be able to offer a new supplier access to a wider market than would be the case with a direct sales force. Unfortunately, however, wholesalers carry a large number of products from many suppliers, and therefore will not be able to give a new product as much individual attention and sales effort as the company marketing effort may require in the initial stage of the launch.

Providing the manufacturer carefully calculates the pricing structure of the product, allowing a sufficient profit margin to be made at each stage of the distribution chain, and backs this with advertising in the media to create a demand from the consumer, wholesalers are the most effective method of ensuring national distribution.

6.4   Wholesale Markets

The distribution of fresh products, meat, fish, vegetables and fruit, is undertaken through wholesale markets controlled by the local authorities of major cities. Individual wholesalers in the market will purchase from importers' agents, packing stations or producers, the wide range of fresh products needed by the population. Goods arrive at the markets throughout the hours of darkness, and are placed on sale before dawn. Retailers, hoteliers and caterers arrive daily to purchase their requirements and the markets have completed their trading by 10.30 am.

6.5   Additional Forms of Distribution

Distribution systems develop to suit the market in which they operate, and in order to fully understand the chain of distribution we need to examine the other methods common in the UK.

Brokers

These act as middlemen between a client and the provider of a service. Brokers are usually found in the areas of share investment and insurance. They act for a number of companies, being paid commission on their dealings, while providing their clients with professional advice on the choice of investment or insurance most likely to meet their needs.

Rack jobbers

This is an American term for suppliers who provide a display stand for placing in an outlet. Goods are merchandised on a regular basis, slow-selling items being replaced with more popular products. Retailer profits are slightly lower using this method, as the stock on display is merchandised on 'sale or return' terms.

Franchisees

A recent development in retail outlets is the franchising of certain areas of the store to specialised distributors. The store wishes to retain a co-ordinated operation, but has neither the skill or expertise to undertake the particular aspect of retailing required. In these cases the management of the outlet will agree to 'rent' an area of the sales floor to a company or individual who will provide both stock and staff to run the operation. Examples are usually jewellers, travel agencies, opticians or exclusive fashion houses.

Voluntary groups

Following the success of supermarket retailing introduced in the early 1960s, independent food retailers found difficulty in competing with the buying power of the supermarket chains. To counter the effect of the supermarkets, lower prices and increased buying power, retailers in similar markets joined together in voluntary groups.

By combining their orders for products, they were able to approach manufacturers and negotiate special prices through wholesalers appointed to service the group members. The voluntary groups have grown in size, and are now able to purchase from manufacturers products packaged under their own brand names, and thus compete in price with the national multiples.

As more independent retailers joined voluntary groups, the groups undertook national advertising and sales promotion. The outlets of members were supplied with restyled shop-fronts, and the interiors refurbished in line with the group image. Voluntary groups in the grocery trade include Spar, Mace and Vivo, and more recently, in the pharmacy market, the Unichem and Vantage groups.

Mail order houses

A growing area of distribution is the mail order house, where products are delivered direct to your home through the postal service or company vehicles. The essential area in mail order operation is in the supply of a full-colour catalogue showing the range of items available. In addition, they offer variable credit terms, monthly payments through agents, and the opportunity to return unsuitable items for replacement or refund.

Advertising for new agents can be seen in popular women's magazines, offering a range of gifts when the agency is opened and initial orders received. Cash commission of 10% is paid to club agents on all orders placed, or 12.5% if taken in the form of goods from the mail order catalogue.

For the housebound the benefits of armchair shopping using the fully-illustrated catalogue overcome the problems of not being able to examine the goods immediately. The free credit terms form an additional advantage in the planning of family purchases.

Direct response distribution

Direct response mail order offers are also to be found in the semi-display columns of all newspapers and many magazines offering books, clothing, stamps and small novelty items. These products, due to bulk purchases made by suppliers, are usually less expensive than those in retail outlets.

Newspaper proprietors, concerned at the increase in fraudulent offers, introduced the Mail Order Protection Scheme (MOPS) to protect their readership. Provided a customer sends payment and an order in direct response to one of these advertisements and the company making the offer fail to deliver within a period of 28 days, the amount paid will be refunded in full by the scheme. The MOPS scheme does not cover companies offering catalogues, demonstrations in the home or visits by sales staff, and customers should be aware of the lack of protection offered.

Newspapers therefore undertake stringent investigations before accepting such advertisements, ensuring the company has sufficient stocks and is properly organised to respond quickly to the large number of orders received through this method of distribution. A recent development in direct response distribution is through the use of Prestel viewdata, allowing orders to be supplied following payment by credit card. Without doubt, future developments in the use of microchip technology will enable orders to be placed directly with suppliers following television advertising.

6.6 Distribution Management

Readers will recall that marketing is interdependent with all the sub-functions of a business, and attempts to retain the correct balance between production, distribution and finance. The alert marketeer will liaise with the different departments of a company to ensure that the marketing needs are understood and implemented. The prevention of departmental rivalries, and the use of clear communication practices, are vital in ensuring customer satisfaction.

The distribution management of an organisation is vital to the marketing function in creating the correct image of a company to the customer. Marketing is involved with the total distribution operation and the areas outlined below are of joint concern to both departments.

Location of distribution depots

Marketing/Sales would probably be happy to have distribution depots in every area where customers exist. Distribution would find a single depot more cost effective. The balance lies between the two extremes, aiming to provide the maximum level of service to customers at the minimum distribution costs.

Figure 6.2 shows examples of common distribution patterns based on the use of either main or satellite depots. The use of a single central depot involves higher transportation costs in moving the goods to the customer, plus the risk of excessive delays. Local depots allow the goods to be distributed more quickly but each depot will have to carry its own stock inventory, thus incurring higher warehouse costs.

Transportation costs

The decision has to be made as to which method of transport will be most suitable. Does the company use road, rail, air or water, and should the required vehicles be operated by the company or contracted to an outside haulier? If the costs of vehicle ownership are taken into account, together with the required additional drivers and administration staff, servicing, garaging, taxation, insurance and replacement expenses, it may prove to be

Fig. 6.2 *Distribution Patterns*

SINGLE MAIN DEPOT DISTRIBUTION

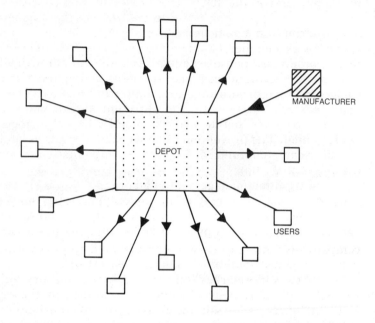

MULTIPLE SATELLITE DEPOTS

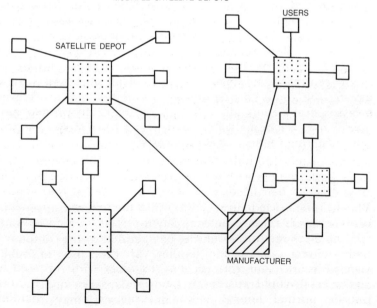

more cost effective to use transport contractors. Adequate journey and drop-size planning is also essential to ensure the maximum use of the fleet. The flexibility and control when operating your own vehicle fleet may outweigh these expenses.

Transport costs could be reduced by negotiating an annual contract with a haulier, based on the amount of traffic generated, or a standard cost per kilo delivered nationwide. Problems may occur with products requiring special handling or transport conditions, together with the ever-present risk of pilferage and damage.

Delivery scheduling

Essential to the management of distribution is the careful consideration of the level of service to be expected by the customer. If delivery schedules fall behind, the consequences can be hazardous in the extreme for the marketing effort of the company. Whatever methods the marketing department of a company may utilise to encourage consumers to purchase, poor delivery and distribution will nullify their efforts.

If a major supermarket company such as Sainsbury did not receive continuous deliveries the store would, in theory, be empty of products for sale within the space of four hours. The length of time required to deliver products is known as the delivery cycle and will vary between product categories. Fresh bread will require a daily delivery cycle, whereas canned goods would possibly only require a 14-day cycle. In order to set the correct service level required by customers, the most important target to decide is the minimum level of orders which our distribution system is expected to deliver and what investment we have to make to achieve this level.

To decide on the number of vehicles we need in our fleet, let us assume that a vehicle can be on the road for a maximum of six hours in a day. In that period of time it could travel approximately 150 miles and make around 15 deliveries. If we have 50 customers within that area who expect delivery daily, then to meet their needs we will require a fleet of four vehicles. We must then decide upon a target for the delivery cycle. Do all our customers require delivery within 24 hours, or would only 95% of them require this level of service? Could we reduce the daily delivery cycle to one offering delivery every three days? Can we reduce our costs by making larger deliveries to less customers? Would customers be willing to accept deliveries outside normal hours? What faster methods of handling products are available? Would customers be prepared to accept palletised loads?

All of these factors must be considered when deciding the correct balance between costs and service levels for our distribution/transport system. Once a target is set for deliveries, marketing can promote the sales benefit to customers. 'Next day delivery – guaranteed' cannot but give confidence to the customer in dealing with the supplier.

Warehousing/storage costs and decisions

Major costs are involved in storing any product, and thus warehousing represents a considerable investment to a company. The first area of investigation is the question as to where the depot should be located. Trading estates of purpose-built warehouses at competitive lease or rental terms have been developed by investment companies and offer companies the opportunity to locate their distribution points close to the motorway network. Internal marketing research will be used to show the location of customers within the distribution area and, if plotted on a map, will illustrate clearly the most suitable location.

Costs for these types of warehouses are determined on the size of the building, and are usually expressed in terms of a rental for each square metre per year. Government policy has been to encourage location of depots in certain areas of the country, and advantageous terms are often available to companies seeking to relocate depots. These may be in the form of tax concessions or rent-free periods, and will all form part of the decision-making process to determine the final location.

The rental costs of premises, however, are not the only expenditure incurred. Insurance, heating, storage equipment, mechanical handling and staff costs are all part of the total costs of operating a distribution point. The stock-holding at individual depots represents a massive investment of capital by the company, and needs careful control and management to ensure that the cost involved does not rise above a certain level. Generally speaking, the stock level should be kept as low as possible, while still retaining customer service levels. Computerised stock control systems allow faster allocation of stock, automatic reordering reports, reduction of inventory, and keep track of order patterns. Future developments in this area will enable suppliers to deal directly with consumers through computerised links, and further reduce inventories.

Physical distribution management

Almost 25% of the total costs involved in marketing a product are expended on the physical distribution segment of the operation. Distribution, for their part, must ensure that the flexibility required for effective marketing is available within the system. Without frequent self-examination distribution can tend to become rigid and unresponsive to changes in the market place.

Regular meetings need to be held between marketing executives and the management of the company's distribution. Covering areas such as product launch dates, projected sales, expected customer offtake, these meetings form a link between the marketing and distribution of the product.

Distribution management undertakes regular reviews, and produces reports, on the amount of stock held. They note slow-selling lines, reporting these to the company management for possible disposal or sales promotion. Where shortfalls in production cause delays in delivery, this also requires reporting to the marketing department so that action can be taken immediately to improve production and notify customers awaiting products.

Distribution is responsible for a large proportion of the company administration and paperwork, which has a direct effect on the service given to customers. Care must be taken to ensure that delivery notes, stock records, internal transfers, invoice requests and special delivery instructions are completed accurately and on time. The marketing effort of the company will be diluted through continued customer complaints, creating a poor company image.

Assignment

Select a single product from each of the following categories and trace the chain of distribution which each product follows from origination to the ultimate consumer or buyer.

1 A manufactured product – e.g. electric toaster.
2 An agricultural product – e.g. English strawberries.
3 An imported product – e.g. Hong Kong soy sauce.

Illustrate your assignment with diagrams of each distribution chain, and give details of each stage and purpose. Details of the additional costs incurred, and the resulting alterations in the final selling-price are to be shown.

Chapter 7
Sales Promotion and Merchandising

The total spent on sales promotion by UK companies in the market place is conservatively estimated at around £8000 million each year, so in this section we are considering one of the major areas of expenditure in marketing.

To describe exactly what should be classed as sales promotion, we refer to this type of expenditure as 'below the line', although many in marketing have little idea as to exactly which line we refer to. The term is supposed to have originated from the bookkeeping departments of advertising agencies who drew a line under all of the clients' charges allocated to the five main types of media:

- Television advertising
- Radio commercials
- Press advertising
- Cinema advertising
- Billboard advertising.

They class this expenditure as being 'above the line' because the agency received a 15% commission from the media concerned. Other forms of media or sales promotion undertaken by agencies are charged at cost, to which the agency will add a handling charge, and therefore are known as 'below the line' expenditure.

Sales promotion is concerned with the variety of methods used to promote a product or service after advertising has taken place, but before the sale. Most sales promotion takes place at or around the point of sale and has a direct appeal to the buyer. Merchandising is often included within sales promotion and, yet again, confusion arises as to the correct definition. Retail merchandising refers to the correct display and stocking of products within a retail outlet, and is not generally seen as part of marketing. The merchandising we conduct in marketing refers to an individual, or series, of short-term promotions designed to boost sales, in response to a particular situation.

7.1 Types of Sales Promotion

Sales promotion usually originates from the manufacturer or supplier of the service, but can equally well be carried out by the seller to promote to the final customer. Sales promotion material consists of consumer leaflets, window display posters and shelf display material, internal and external permanent signs, short-term display stands, window display items which can often demonstrate or supply movement to the product, samples, testers, dummy bottles and cans, and a wide variety of plastic and paper carriers.

Consumer leaflets

Provided free of charge by the manufacturer of the product for use by sales staff, or for attaching to shelving in specially designed holders, these give technical and usage information to the customer. They may consist of a simple two-colour typeset A5 leaflet, right through to a comprehensive brochure showing the range of products, illustrated by full-colour photographs of the product in use.

Display posters and shelf display materials

As the number of sales assistants employed in retailing decreased, so the importance of display materials and posters increased. Eventually the proliferation of vivid fluorescent billboards in every retail outlet reached such a pitch that planning regulations were introduced to restrict the amount allowed.

The provision of display posters by suppliers, together with a wide variety of shelf 'talkers' and 'wobblers', forms a major part of a company's sales promotion. Usually supplied free of charge by manufacturers, they ensure that the products catch the attention of the consumer. Research has shown that the average amount of time taken by a shopper in deciding to purchase a product when in a retail grocery outlet is less than four seconds. Shelf display materials are just one of the ways of ensuring that a new product gains the maximum attention needed to succeed.

Internal and external permanent signs

Larger national manufacturers will supply a number of permanent signs for use in the retail outlet. These may consist of a complete fascia, or front, for the outlet, where the supplier's brand name, logo or advertising message is given equal prominence with the trading name of the shop. Extensively used in the petrol industry, and CTN (confectionery, tobacco and news) outlets, they form a long-term sales promotion for the supplier. Internal permanent signs can be in the form of display frames and boards, electronic clocks, mobile turntables, or simple open/closed signs, each bearing the company message or logo.

Short-term display stands

This is often the most impressive type of display seen in the retail outlet, and it is sometimes difficult to realise that they often only consist of screen-printed card, plastic or wood, produced in large quantities at a relatively low cost. Likewise, stands showing selections of cosmetics for consumer testing, each item carefully positioned, complete with mirrors, appear to be constructed of solid marble, but on examination prove to be nothing more than thin moulded plastic. From the simplest package carton, which when carefully cut forms a display unit, to the most substantial-looking display rack, these are all examples of the art of producing short-term sales promotion.

Window display items

Many products have features which are difficult to illustrate, and thus would benefit from being demonstrated. Manufacturers use considerable ingenuity in providing window display items which will convince the consumer of the benefits offered by the product. Examples include the watertight watch busily working under a constant flow of water, the vacuum cleaner supporting a beach ball, and the video camera pointing towards the passing shopper. Movement within a window display is certain to grab the attention of the consumer, confirmed by the many turntables and swinging-type signs provided.

Samples, testers, dummies

Sampling of the product is common in all product areas, allowing customers to either handle, test or demonstrate the product in use. Retailers are well aware that once a product has been handled, the sale becomes considerably easier to make. Small samples of products in the DIY market allow consumers to return home and check colour correctness. The importance of this is illustrated by paint and wall-covering manufacturers now supplying miniature pots or swatches at special low prices, the cost being refundable when purchasing the larger container or roll.

Testers in the cosmetic and perfumery market are essential, depending as it does purely on personal preference. The heaviest weight of advertising placed behind a brand is reinforced by the opportunity to sample.

In the past, dummy products produced for display were a major part of sales promotion, and all manufacturers supplied large quantities. However, many no longer do so, finding the cost of supplying an empty container is often higher than supplying a full one.

7.2   Merchandising

The short-term promotion of a product at the point of sale offers the management of the brand a wide range of inexpensive methods to boost sales. The reasons for deciding to undertake a sales-promotion merchandising scheme might be the following:

1   to successfully launch a new product on the market
2   as a boost to flagging sales turnover
3   to counter competitive activity
4   to encourage distributors to increase stock levels
5   as a lesser cost alternative to media advertising
6   to increase customer awareness and build brand loyalty.

Schemes can be extremely simple, requiring nothing more than an alteration to the packaging or pricing of a product in a single outlet, through to complicated nationally organised promotions supported by massive marketing efforts.

Coupons or vouchers

As an effective sales promotion scheme the coupon offer is a well-tried and tested method of boosting sales, or encouraging new product purchase. Recommended as one of the less expensive types of promotion, it should be borne in mind that at the simplest level the only expenditure needed in this purely 'paper promotion' is the printing of a suitable voucher or coupon. The basic idea behind a voucher is to distribute to the public a printed coupon offering a discount on their purchase. It can be undertaken by the smallest corner store or self-employed person, provided simple marketing and legal points are understood.

Figure 7.1 shows a typical voucher, which can be distributed to local households, possibly by the members of a youth group or scout troop, or by insertion in a newspaper or free sheet. As the voucher has a high perceived value by the recipient, the likely result is that it will be carefully saved for later use, forming a continuous reminder of the product and company making the offer. The points to note, by reference to the illustration, are as follows:

1   value of coupon clearly stated for use against goods;
2   expiry date shown, to prevent late redemption;
3   minimum   purchase   shown   to   prevent   multiple redemption;
4   discount off purchases only (no cash value);
5   sequentially numbered and/or coded by area, to show redemption rate from each distribution area.

Fig. 7.1 *Example Discount Voucher*

Remember that the better the quality of paper and printing used, the higher the consumer values the voucher. Many companies produce vouchers which in many aspects resemble bank notes or cheques. Redemption rates vary, but in general can be expected to be around 5% of the vouchers distributed, so stockists must ensure that sufficient quantities of the product are available to meet the anticipated up-take.

Vouchers can also be printed in daily newspapers or specialist magazines, offering reductions at certain outlets or from a particular brand. While the general design of the voucher follows a similar pattern to Figure 7.1 the method of redemption is different. For example, once a consumer has used the voucher in the correct way, the vouchers are forwarded in bulk to a number of coupon-handling companies, who forward a cheque or credit voucher for their value to the retailer or supermarket head office, in addition to a handling charge.

Malredemption can be a problem for those manufacturers using coupons, as many large retailers discount against any product they stock. In an attempt to prevent this, some are turning to the refund of the voucher face value on return of proof of purchase.

Banded multiple or jumbo packs

To increase brand share we can promote through the sale of packs which band together more than one of a product. These packs are then offered at a reduced price compared with the combined cost of single products. Adhesive tape or Netlon bags printed with special offer signs attract consumer purchase, with the added advantage that at the close of the promotion the product can be returned to the original form simply by removing the tape or bags. By selling multiple packs, the competition is denied future as well as present sales. Customers have a limit to the amount of product they can consume, so by purchasing a multiple pack – for example a pack of three soap bars – the need to repurchase is delayed and the competition suffers.

Jumbo packs of products offering extra 'free' product have the same effect, but concern is being felt that eventually the consumer will be unable to judge what is a normal pack, the jumbo having become the expected size.

Dealer competitions

Usually related to the purchase of stock, care has to be taken that they do not contravene the legal sanctions seeking to prevent the corruption of retail or industrial buyers. In general, the prizes must be allocated on the basis of chance, and not won solely by purchasing the required quantity.

Consumer competitions

A competition intended for the consumer will require the return of part of the product pack as proof of purchase, together with an entry form. The advantage lies in the often forgotten fact that however many entries are submitted, only a predetermined number of prizes are being offered and thus costs are fixed at the commencement of the promotion. If the competition catches the eye of the consumer and a large number of entries are received, the cost per product sold is greatly reduced. A recent competition held at Luton Airport for departing travellers using the facilities attracted 250 000 entries for the major prize – a five-door hatchback saloon car: a cost equivalent of less than three pence per thousand entries. The resultant publicity when the vehicle was presented gave an added bonus to the organisers.

The major prize must be sufficiently attractive to encourage entry, with minor consolation prizes for as many entries as possible within the budget. The competition should hold the attention of the entrant, which does not necessarily mean that the prize itself must be of high value, but rather that the form of competition should require an element of skill. If possible, the questions should be so arranged as to give what appears to be a fair chance of winning, with a tie-breaker, usually in the form of a suitable slogan, determining the final winner.

To ensure fairness, a suitable panel of judges drawn from a number of areas – media, company, distributors or trade assoc-iations – should be asked to oversee the final judging. A final date for entries should be given, which should be closely followed by the announcement of the winners. Too long a delay between entry and results causes intense suspicion, and can lead to prob-lems with the Advertising Standards Authority, who are quite prepared to take suitable action against those who offend. The normal method of announcement of winners is through the *Competitors' Journal* or by offering to provide a full listing on request.

After-use packaging

A useful promotion appealing to the collecting instinct of the consumer, this leads to continued product purchase in order to 'make the set'. Not all products are suitable for this type of promotion, but the marketing executive should consider if the product could be packaged within a container which offers an after-use. Examples include coffee jars, which with the addition of a label form general storage containers, ice cream containers used for lunch pails, and pâté containers used as kitchen ware. Given a little thought, almost any product can be packaged in this way, increasing the apparent value of the product.

Self-liquidating premiums

In return for special proofs of purchase taken from the product pack, and a nominal payment, an attractive, exclusive and bargain-priced item is sent by post to the customer. By purchasing in bulk, or commissioning an item from a supplier and without wishing to make a profit, marketing is able to pass the resultant saving on to the customer.

When starting the offer, care has to be taken that the specially marked packs are actually in stock at the point of sale, and that sufficient products are available to meet the demand. Should the demand exceed stocks, customers should be contacted and either offered a similar value product, or a return of monies paid. Both these problems are quite common, and insurance policies can now be taken out to cover this eventuality and the possible consequences.

Chapter 8

Advertising

The Codfish lays ten thousand eggs,
The Hen lays only one,
But the Codfish never cackles,
To tell you what she's done,
And so we scorn the Codfish,
But the lowly Hen we prize,
Which clearly goes to show you,
It pays to advertise!

Advertising can be selling made visible.

An average TV advertisement lasts for 30 seconds, and allows up to fourteen million viewers the opportunity to view a new company product: enough to fill Wembley Stadium 250 times over . . .

Advertising can be inspiring/uplifting.

MEN WANTED for hazardous journey. Small wages, bitter cold, long months of complete darkness, constant danger, safe return doubtful. Honour and recognition in case of success.
(*Reputed to have been used by Sir Ernest Shackleton when recruiting for his polar expedition.*)

Advertising can seek to prevent – or to promote.

'If you drink – don't drive' . . . (*every year since 1970*).
'AIDS – you know the risks – the decision is yours' . . . (*every year until 19—?*)

Advertising can seek to persuade.

'Tingle fresh Gibbs S.R.' ... (*first UK commercial TV advertisement*).

Advertising exists to encourage the customer to buy, rather than simply inform, and it is this element of persuasion which makes the industry of such importance to marketing. In this chapter we will examine the advantages and disadvantages of each of the different media, so that those involved in marketing or advertising can judge which method offers the most effective means of promoting their product or service to the buyer.

In the world of advertising the creative staff who first conceive the advertisement, write the advertising copy, decide the most suitable media to use and test the completed advertisement are paid high salaries and bonus payments to produce that winning campaign. Despite their best efforts, advertising is still risky business, where considerable amounts of money are expended in the belief that sales of the favoured product will increase.

8.1   Criticisms of Advertising

The marketing student will quickly discover that advertising is one of the major aspects of marketing which attracts considerable adverse comment. These criticisms are normally centred upon the effect of advertising on the consumer, on the young, on the increased costs incurred, and on the whole question of ethics in advertising.

Advertisements are often blamed for persuading consumers to buy what they don't need, what they shouldn't have and what they can't afford. This is a classic case of killing the messenger because the message is unpopular. Advertising does not add significantly to the cost of production, as the purpose is to ensure that sales should increase in the short term, and hopefully retain that increase over a longer period once the advertising campaign is completed.

Advertisements are accused of being false, deceptive, misleading and one-sided by those who seek to further control the media. However, the continued use of legal controls by trading standards officers, and the efforts of the advertising industry to regulate itself are reducing the number of legitimate complaints with a corresponding improvement in the image of the profession.

Advertisers are often thought able to influence editorial independence. It is assumed that advertisers investing heavily in a particular medium will expect any unfavourable references to their products to be removed. But even with a major spending advertiser it is doubtful if they will attempt to concern themselves with the editorial content. Only when a medium loses popularity with the buyer will action be taken – by transferring the advertising budget to a competitor giving higher readership. Advertisers are interested purely in a sales return for their money, and will judge advertising media by the sales which result for the advertisement.

Television has all the advantages of a near-perfect advertising medium. TV reaches the mass market; it can portray movement and can appeal to both sight and hearing. But with so many advertising media competing for the buyer's attention, it is no surprise to discover that commercial breaks on television still present an opportunity to make a 'quick cuppa'. This has become such a fixed habit by the consumer that electricity and water utilities keep notes of the schedules ready to meet the sudden upsurge in demand as three million kettles are filled and switched on.

Television is not the only medium which suffers from lack of attention. Research commissioned by newspapers which showed that 20% of the total readership never glance at a single advert, 50% glance at the page but read no further, and only 30% read the advert. In view of this singular lack of attention on the part of the buyers, the role of the advertising agency becomes of even greater importance.

8.2   Available Media

No-one in marketing need complain about a lack of media available for advertising. The list below contains the popular advertising media, and also the wider variety of specialised advertising outlets. As in other marketing disciplines, it is not always the best policy to follow the herd, slavishly pursuing the same methods as competitors. Far better to carefully consider where the most effective advertising may be placed to gain maximum sightings by the required customers. However, the seven media below are commonly accepted as the first choice for advertising campaigns.

Popular consumer media
- television
- radio
- cinema
- daily, weekly and national papers

- weekly magazines
- poster sites
- free sheets.

Useful for specific market segments, and often less costly, are these

Specialist media
- trade magazines and papers
- agricultural market poster sites
- public transport shelter sites
- parking meter advertising
- taxicab advertising
- public telephone advertising
- van and transport advertising
- rail advertising
- air transport advertising
- sea transport advertising
- video advertising.

8.3 Advertising Costs

Advertising is normally charged by the media concerned on the basis of the space used, the length of time taken, or in some cases by a combination of both. Looking at the comparative costs of advertising, before making a choice of how to allocate our budget, we find that there are in fact four different methods of calculating the cost of each medium. As in all aspects of business it is not always the simple comparisons which will give the full picture, but rather deeper considerations are needed before choosing the correct advertising media.

Comparative cost

A simple cost comparison between types of media may prove useful in determining how far the advertising budget can be spread. If the budget is limited, then choices will have to be made as to which will produce the most effective return for the lowest cost. It is not always easy to decide if the expenditure on a fairly short TV advertising campaign would produce a more effective response than a year-long campaign in a specialist trade magazine. Comparative cost merely quantifies the various costs of the media, but gives no measure of effectiveness.

Cost per reader/viewer

A far better method than a simple comparison is to measure the effectiveness of the media based on the number of readers or viewers who could possibly be exposed to the advertisement. By dividing the cost of the time or space taken by the total number of readers or viewers, we arrive at a figure which we can then use as a true comparison cost between the different media.

Example

Local free sheet   – half-page advertisement £300
ABC readership   60 000
Cost per reader $\dfrac{30\ 000}{60\ 000}$ p

Therefore cost per reader = 0.5 pence

Cost for total readership

Certain media, because of their perceived value or usefulness, are retained by the buyer for a longer period. During this extended period a number of further opportunities are created for the advertisement to be read. While this further readership is often difficult to quantify, nevertheless it must play a part in deciding the effective cost per reader. Typical of the type of media with a strong retention factor are trade directories, television magazines, *International Reader's Digest*, etc.

The advertising in this type of media offers a repeat factor, which in effect reduces the cost per reader of the advert. Many magazines and periodicals can have a total readership some ten times greater than the circulation figures may suggest.

Cost per reader/viewer in the correct market segment

Advertising expenditure is only effective if it appeals to the correct customer segment of the particular market in which the company operates. Media operators will supply a breakdown of their viewing or readership patterns to show which particular segment of the market is covered. The example given in Figure

8.1 is based on the Midlands UK area, and shows the audience figures for certain demographic sections.

Fig. 8.1 *Example of Audience Categories and Coverage – Midlands Area*

Audience Category	% share cover
1 Housewives	7.00%
2 Housewives + children	8.69%
3 Adults	8.47%
4 Men	10.5%
5 Women	7.84%
6 Adults 16-24 years age group	18.5%
7 Men 16-34 years age group	15.38%
8 ABC1 Adults	10.8%
9 ABC1 Men	12.5%

(Source: BRMB Radio)

8.4 Buying and Booking Advertising Space/Time

British Rate and Data (BRAD) is the essential reference book for all media buying and booking, giving regularly updated costings, together with accurate details of circulation or viewing figures. The required format for advertising copy is also given, together with details of the reservation procedures and final dates for copy. Consulting this volume helps the marketeer calculate, using the methods in the previous section, the most suitable choice of media based on purely factual information.

The Blue Book of British Broadcasting gives full programme information on every radio or TV channel in the UK and enables advertisers to target accurately for maximum impact. When booking space on commercial television it will produce a far greater impact if the products are advertised at the beginning or end of a relevant programme. Advertisements for toys, games and related products will be shown during children's programmes in the full expectation that this type of programme is likely to attract our target market.

Warning

We must always consider who is the true customer. Very often a product would appear to have an appeal to a particular market segment, such as the children's toys mentioned above. Although, at first, it may appear that the true market segment is indeed children, it only takes a moment to realise that the true customer could well be the parent, or indeed a grandparent, purchasing the product as a gift. Would it therefore not be better to advertise in a medium read or viewed by that segment?

8.5   The Advertising Agency

For 140 years from 1712 to the mid-1800s the government of the day taxed newspaper advertisements, reducing the amount of advertising carried out by legitimate business. When the tax was removed, suddenly newspaper publishers realised that the new methods of mass production and fast distribution required an equally fast advertising system. There came upon the scene the 'space salesman' who sold the advertising on behalf of the publisher, and was paid a commission for his success. Publishers found this an easier way of conducting their business, as they could pass the task of controlling and checking the dates, positioning of adverts, etc., into the hands of the 'space salesman'.

It was not long before a far-sighted 'space salesman' realised that if he bought the advertising on his own account, then he could 'retail' this to the advertisers, and make himself a greater amount of profit. Newspapers were happy, for their space was being sold in larger blocks, advertisers were happy as they could negotiate discounts. Only the poor salesman had to work harder as the competition latched on to the idea.

From this developed the advertising agencies which we see today, undertaking the total advertising campaign on behalf of their clients, offering a wide range of services and ensuring that the objectives of their clients' marketing campaign are met. Most large advertisers utilise an agency in preference to carrying out the differing functions with their own staff, even though savings in cost could be made. The reason for this is the considerably wider knowledge gained by an agency through their involvement in various sectors. The individual expertise built up by members of the agency staff is the determining factor in ensuring that an agency is a success.

The smaller company wishing to run a short advertising campaign will soon discover that few, if any, of the larger London-based advertising agencies would be prepared to undertake to control the smaller budget. They will find it far easier to contact one of the many agencies in every major city, who would be happy to give the attention and interest the smaller client requires. However, there is nothing to prevent the smaller advertisers booking their own space requirements, provided they conform to the media terms of trade. Negotiating the best possible series discounts, or any other spot rates which may apply, is a difficult task for those lacking experience. The Association of Media Independents acts on behalf of the smaller advertiser, negotiating terms on their behalf, and passing on the discounts obtained to the customer.

In general we need to check the advertising strategy by answering the following four questions:

1   Which customers will have most influence on the decision to buy my product or service?
2   What do they read, listen to, or view?
3   When will they be most likely to make the buying decision?
4   Where will the buying decision be made?

Organisation of the advertising agency

Each agency will be organised on different lines, but most will structure themselves into:
- Account management and planning department
- Creative department
- Media department
- Traffic and production department.

However, clients will not deal with their agencies through individual departments, but rather through the account executive who acts as a contact point between the client and the agency. The account executive co-ordinates the efforts of the individual departments of the agency, in addition to ensuring that the client is kept fully informed of progress, usually through a series of regular meetings.

Account management and planning

With such a diverse range of functions within an agency there is certainly a need for the planning and co-ordination of the client account within the agency. It used to be that account executives functioned primarily to entertain clients. However, as costs rose and the number of staff employed in the agencies fell, so the task of the account manager became of greater importance to co-ordinate the range of activities carried out in the agency, and by outside specialists.

If a client had to consult with the different sectors within the agency, then a considerable amount of time and effort would be wasted by both the agency staff and the brand management of the client company. Account management takes away this problem, ensuring that the brand management is consulted on all aspects of the campaign planning.

The planning function in an agency is carried out by trained researchers, whose responsibility is to ensure that the decisions made by the brand manager and the account manager during their discussions on the campaign are backed up by reasoned and accurate research. Agencies will in some cases continue to refer to this post as that of researcher.

Fig. 8.2 *Advertising Agency Account Group*

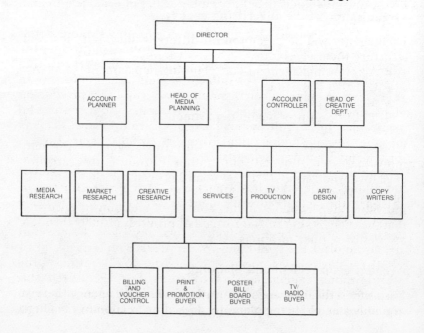

ADVERTISING AGENCY ACCOUNT GROUP

The creative department

Together the client brand manager and the account manager will write the campaign brief. A campaign brief is the background information on the product as it is marketed at present, the future marketing objectives of the brand, and an outline of the proposals for achieving those objectives.

The creative department then takes over the brief and concentrates on producing the 'actual' advertisements which consist of pictures and copy. This department is where the true creativity takes place, and is usually under the control of the creative director, working in conjunction with different teams of experts. Copywriters are employed to produce the 'wordage' of the advertisements, including the slogans and headlines. Copy is the selling part of the advertisement, as against the attention-getting aspects of the headline and pictures. Many famous authors have at times been employed as coypwriters in advertising agencies before finding fame and fortune writing fiction!

Countless drafts and alterations are produced before the campaign advertising begins to take shape, but once the process is completed, then the creative department will undertake the production of the advertisement. The larger the agency the more likely this function is to be carried out using internal production facilities.

Large agencies will have a number of executives whose duties will include the purchase of the required facilities to produce the advert. Art studios will produce print-ready artwork, casting departments will search for suitable models or actors for use in television or film advertisements, and the TV production department will undertake liaison with production film companies. Just as copywriters move on to achieve fame, so many of the Oscar-winning film directors began their careers producing TV advertisements!

With the smaller agency – size being calculated on the total of the billings undertaken by the agency over all media – the task of creating the actual advertisement is undertaken by outside specialists who concentrate their skills and attention in one particular area. These production facilities allow the smallest agency to offer the same range of services as the larger.

Advertising is based on success. The agency that produces the world-beating campaign will attract further clients. In this respect it is the ideas and ability of the creative director that form the mainstay of the agency. Head-hunting is common amongst all agencies, with creative staff being encouraged to transfer between competing agencies, in the hope that the client will follow. Creative staff will break away from their present agency to form other specialised agencies, with a limited client base.

The media department

Selection and negotiation of discounts, space, series discount, together with booking and arranging space in a medium is the responsibility of this department within an agency. Media planners are involved in the decision as to which media will present the most effective use of the advertising budget, and in the buying of the required space or time. As each medium became more specialised in catering for the advertiser, so the demand grew for specialists who could, through their greater knowledge, negotiate with the media providers over each series of advertisements.

Price is dependent upon timing and positioning, granting of discounts for a series of insertions, special promotional deals, or simple demand. Researchers will have available the market data for each medium, to assist the creative department in achieving the objectives of the client brief.

Traffic and production

Brilliant ideas! Wonderful artwork! Creative expertise! All are useless if the traffic and production department do not carry out their essential duties.

Each medium requires notification in advance of the agency's requirements – modern printing and production requires considerable lead times. Magazine printing requires colour separation plates to be made available, each taking considerable time and effort to produce. Copy deadlines for national or weekend newspapers are usually set at six weeks before date of publication.

The whole campaign could falter because of a simple failure to book space in advance of needs. Advertising copy and artwork must be available in a number of different formats to meet the media requirements. All this is the responsibility of the traffic and production department.

Account group

The different functions of the full service agency come together in the form of an account group whose responsibility is to oversee the direction of the campaign brief. In a small agency this could be the account director, a media person (planner/ negotiator), the creative group, and a representative from traffic and production.

Brand management within the client company will be collecting data on sales, throughout the period of the campaign, from their sales force, and will meet regularly with the account group to discuss progress. Sales feedback from the company is essential and will have an influence on which aspect of the campaign needs alteration or a change in strategy.

8.6 The Development of Specialised Agencies and Media Independents

For many years the car owner expected full service from his local main garage, calling for a service, petrol, tyre replacement, body repairs and washing. Gradually the market spread, with specialists entering the field, until we now have the situation where the car owner is prepared to visit a specialised tyre and exhaust outlet, a body repair shop, a service shop, and to purchase petrol alone at a local filling station.

This situation has become common in the field of advertising, with specialist media independents buying on behalf of clients, taking a lower commission rate on the media billing and passing back the remaining commission to the client. Production companies now tend to specialise in various markets and have taken over certain functions from full service agencies, with financial, direct response, sales promotion and publicity agencies offering a restricted range of services, each with highly concentrated knowledge and skills. They offer client companies a unique understanding of their product or promotion method, and with this can effectively compete with the full-service agencies.

8.7 Newspaper Advertising

The United Kingdom has nine national daily newspapers, together with over 13 600 regional weekly and daily newspapers, representing one of the largest single nationwide mass media methods of marketing in the world. While TV is seen as the most effective medium by many outside marketing organisations, it remains the most expensive in cost terms. A sum three times greater than all TV expenditure combined is spent by advertisers each year on newspaper and regional press advertising.

Benefits of newspaper advertising

Newspapers provide a similar spread of national coverage to television, together with the added advantage of having specific types of readership available. Socio-economic groupings do tend to read and purchase specific newspapers, almost to the exclusion of all others. Despite the humour which has arisen as to origins of the '*Sun* Reader', whose interest is purely in the third page, 6% of readers do belong to the top A and B social group, which still compares badly with *The Times* figure of 55%. However, the groupings for the mass marketing of products is best served by the national tabloid daily, having some 70% of the population as readership.

Methods of newspaper advertising

National newspaper advertising campaigns are placed by the company advertising agency, and the booking of space varies little from that involved in regional advertising. The major difficulty in regional advertising lies in advertisers having to contact individual regional papers, reserve space for the identical campaign time, supply similar artwork to all the regions, and change factors such as branch addresses in each paper. To overcome this problem the newspaper proprietors have formed the Newspaper Advertising Bureau, which allows bookings to be made on a regional basis. The free sheet papers have matched this with the formation of the Association of Free Newspapers based in Gloucester. However, the practitioner of marketing should be aware of the background and familiar with the methods used in designing and conducting a campaign in the local press. This is more than likely the first medium with which he or she will be actively involved.

Reasons for advertising

Before any advertising is undertaken, we must be aware of why the campaign is being run. To advertise merely to keep abreast of the competition is not sufficient reason in itself. The reasons must relate to the medium being used. If using a local weekly newspaper we do not attempt to advertise national brands or products, but keep the product information and offers relevant to the local market.

Examine the style of advert offered in a national newspaper, and compare the content, layout and message with identical full-page advertisements in your local paper or free sheet. The local paper will have a distinctly parochial flavour with the advertisement concentrating on selling the benefits of the product or service, rather than expanding the image of the company by 'corporate' advertising. Local newspaper advertising will be used for the following reasons:

1   to announce new products, new business ventures or new sales promotions;
2   to retain the interest and attention of existing clients and customers;
3   to produce enquiries or responses for services or products;
4   to create company or brand awareness.

The reason why many advertisements fail to achieve their full selling potential is because inexperienced advertisers seek to include all the areas in one single advert, creating confusion in the mind of a reader.

Key factors in carrying out newspaper advertising

1   The message must be clearly stated.
2   It must immediately attract the attention of the reader.
3   The advert should reappear, wherever possible, at the same position within the paper.
4   Supply clear pictures or line drawings of the product.
5   Sell benefits in the copywriting.
6   Advertisements must include price, sale price, savings.
7   Advertisements must be easy to understand and read.
8   Include related items.
9   Check the timing by noting the results obtained.
10   Check proof copy each time.
11   If it works once – use it again.
12   Advertise frequently – small but often.
13   Decide a joint advertising/promotion plan in advance.
14   Decide a local newspaper advertising budget.
15   Never advertise in joint promotions.

Fig. 8.3   *Newspaper Advertising Sizes and Positions*

DISPLAY ⅛th PAGE

SINGLE
COLUMN
PER
CM

FOR SALE: Tricity 6 cu. ft. chest freezer, perfect working order. ☎ Cummertrees 359.

GENYK large bird cage, as new, 14″ x 25 x 21″ height, £30. ☎ Dumfries 68350 evenings.

LADY'S Pathfinder boys 'Puch' racer bikes, both good condition, £50 each. ☎ Annan 4254.

LARCH LAP fencing, built and erected to customers requirements. Free estimates. ☎ Annan 5185.

MARMET coachbuilt pram, navy / white, shopping tray, sun canopy, ex. condition, £60. ☎ Annan 3625.

GEORGE F. SIMMONS & CO.
CARLYLE'S PLACE, ANNAN
For all PLUMBING and HEATING INSTALLATIONS.
REPAIRS and MAINTENANCE
also
BATHROOMS and KITCHENS
by leading manufacturers
D.I.Y. MATERIALS

OFFICE OPEN
Monday to Friday
9 a.m. - 12.00 a.m.
1.30 p.m. to 4.30 p.m.

TELEPHONE
Annan 2767
and 5320

DOUBLE COLUMN
PER CM X 2

BORDER WINDOWS
for your uPVC window
and door requ...
Front d...

PREFERRED POSITION

CJs
HAIRDRESSING
and **GIFT SHOP**
NOW OPEN
ALL DAY ON
WEDNESDAY

HAIR
SALON

130 HIGH ST. ANNAN
Tel. 2527

ANNANDALE
Observer
No. 6567   MEMBER OF THE DUMFRIESSHIRE NEWSPAPER GROUP
Registered at the Post Office as a Newspaper
Friday, 24th June, 1988   Price 24p

Bairds
for
PRAMS
£10 Deposit
secures
with free
mattress and
pillow

RESIDENTS COUNTER

RESIDENTS ON an estate in Annan are fighting back against the vandals and hooligans who have been making their lives miserable for years.
A large group of them have sent a letter to Dumfries and Galloway's Chief Constable, John Boyd and Dumfriesshire's MP, Sir Hec-

ATTACK

Successful advertising is a combination of these tried and tested rules, together with the confidence to keep advertising when things are going well or badly. Regular advertising which keeps the name of the company in the mind of the customer, even though the advertisement is small in size, is far more effective than large pages of advertising run infrequently.

8.8   Television Advertising

Short of a salesperson's visit, or the customer attending a live demonstration, there is nothing more suitable than television advertising for showing how a product works. Television has the advantage of being able to portray movement, colour and sound in the home of the potential customer under the most relaxing of circumstances. The average viewer spends around three hours every day watching television and during that time might be exposed to some 18 minutes of commercial breaks.

Henry Ford once said that 50% of all advertising is wasted – but no one knows which 50%! Television, of all the media, has one of the lowest wastage factors. Apart from the loss incurred through transmitting advertisements which have little appeal to the particular viewer, the only other problem is that the rate of retention is very low. Many consumers happily recall the words, the jingle, the tune, the actors, but fail totally to recall the product names.

In 30 seconds the advertisement has to get across the ideas and benefits of a product, and carry this out in such a way that the target consumers retain this information until next visiting a retail outlet, or being in a position where they are ready to purchase.

Television plays a part in building a new product – provided it forms part of a comprehensive advertising package. Used as a single medium it will not be successful. It can only form part of a campaign together with poster, press and sales promotion, etc.

In the United Kingdom we have at present only two commercial channels split into 15 different regions. Each region operates in conjunction with others in carrying advertising breaks, and it should be possible to run a single advertisement nationally at a total cost for 30 seconds of around £140 000. In practice a television advertisement is normally shown in a limited number of regions, based on the principle that a budget is better spent in a concentrated burst of advertising rather than a lesser series spread throughout the nation. With a solus campaign carried out in a single area the company would normally offer a substantial discount on published cost schedules.

Advertisers measure the results obtained by means of television rating points (TVRs), each single point representing 35 000 homes who can be expected to be watching a programme when the advertisement is screened. By calculating the number of TVR ratings each commercial break provides, it is a simple matter to construct a target viewing audience, and from this calculate the number of advertisements required.

Research is carried out by the questioning of a sample of viewers to discover opinions on programmes viewed during the previous seven days, and in addition by the installation of electronic meters in a representative sample of 3000 homes, covering over 7500 individuals aged over four years old. The meter transmits data of television usage to a central computer each night. This audience measurement data is then made available to advertisers and agencies on payment of a subscription charge. From this audience research the advertiser can calculate the number of each demographic group watching the particular commercial breaks.

Additional information from the commercial station includes the Consumer Audit, providing a panel of householders who record purchases made during the week. The audit provides information on the actual behaviour of the purchaser, and acceptance of the product.

One of the more interesting types of survey is the 'dustbin' survey, where researchers collect every single label, package and container used by the household during a set period. TV companies find this most useful in assessing consumption rates and purchase patterns.

Analysis of all the data obtained provides information on:

* weekly purchasing patterns;
* brand profiles;
* repeat purchasing;
* brand share;
* switching between competing brands;
* usage of product;
* coupon redemption;
* effectiveness of free samples and special promotions.

To reach a particular market the advertiser will decide upon a target television rating, and by simple calculation decide the number of commercials needed to be broadcast to reach the target group.

> **Example**
>
> 300 TVR for teenagers – Programme rating 10 TVR, therefore number of transmissions required is 300/10 = 30.

Restrictions on television advertising

One of the signs showing the strength of television advertising in altering our buying habits is the lengthy list of restrictions placed upon advertisers and advertisements by the Independent Broadcasting Authority.

Television will never be allowed as part of the media campaign plans of the following list of business ventures:

- (i) breath-testing devices;
- (ii) products masking the effects of alcohol;
- (iii) matrimonial agencies;
- (iv) fortune tellers;
- (v) racing tipsters;
- (vi) undertakers;
- (vii) private detectives;
- (ix) cigarettes and cigarette tobacco.

Severe restrictions are placed upon the advertising style, including the use of advertisements calculated to produce fear in the mind of the viewer. Adverts appealing to children carry a wide number of rules, one of the most significant being the requirement to clearly show which toys are powered purely by imagination!

In addition to this list of banned products or services the representatives of the IBA, the Independent Television Companies Association and the programme companies will view all television commercials before transmission. Advertisements from local companies will be checked by the TV company local sales manager to ensure that the above restrictions are not contravened, but also to ensure that advertisers are not attempting to run a national campaign through local dealerships, to take advantage of the much reduced rates offered to local clients.

Purchasing transmission time

Available in a variety of formats and timings, we can purchase television advertising in multiples of ten-second slots, with the average advertisement being of 30 seconds duration. A variety of rates are available dependent upon series bookings, special agreements and commercial negotiations.

Advertisers are prevented from using advertisements that have some form of relationship, either in the content, in the use of television stars on screen, or as 'voice overs', within two hours of any programme in which they have appeared.

Most local advertisements are placed at competitive rates, when compared with the rates required for national advertisers. The rate card shown in figure 8.4 is the 1988 rate card for Central TV showing the different rates for each ten-second section.

Fig. 8.4   *Central TV Rate Card*

CENTRAL
1988 RATECARD
ITV & CHANNEL 4
Effective 1st January 1988

SPOT TYPE	10 SEC	20 SEC	30 SEC	40 SEC	50 SEC	60 SEC
CFR	9350	15520	18700	24930	31150	32730
D10	8415	13968	16830	22437	28035	29457
D20	7480	12416	14960	19944	24920	26184
D30	6545	10864	13090	17451	21805	22911
D40	5610	9312	11220	14958	18690	19638
D50	4675	7760	9350	12465	15575	16365
D60	3740	6208	7480	9972	12460	13092
D70	2805	4656	5610	7479	9345	9819
D75	2338	3880	4675	6233	7788	8183
D80	1870	3104	3740	4986	6230	6546
D85	1403	2328	2805	3740	4673	4910
D90	935	1552	1870	2493	3115	3273
D95	468	776	935	1247	1558	1637
ITV ROC	325	540	650	865	1079	1138
CH4 ROC	225	375	450	600	750	790

Example

A national company – Cadbury – running a national campaign, would have to invest £20 000 for a 40-second advertisement (see Spot type D20) to be played during the showing of a popular James Bond movie or the FA Cup Final. The local advertiser would pay £865 for a 40-second (ITV Run Of Campaign) advertisement aimed at their local market sector probably shown after 24.00 hours (at the company's choice).

Future developments in television advertising

Television advertising expenditure continues to grow, doubling in size every six years – reaching a total expenditure of £1.675 million in 1986. The development in satellite and cable television presents a new and challenging area of development, with both presenting the marketing manager with the opportunity to target advertising at particular buyers in specific market segments.

8.9   Commercial Independent Radio

The only medium without a visual impact, nevertheless radio has an immediacy which other advertising cannot match. Unlike many media which have to distract the consumer in order to gain attention, radio is the only medium appealing to individual listeners while they continue with their normal activities.

Radio operates within distinct time-scales, prime time or 'drive-time' being from Monday-Friday 0700-0900 when the highest listening figures occur. Radio is by nature of the equipment and design a local-based advertising medium, equivalent in style to the weekly local newspaper. Over 55% of the population of the UK gain their first news of the day through the medium of radio. Specific market groups can be selected because at different times of the day a radio audience can be clearly defined, as follows:

TIME SCALE	AUDIENCE
Early morning listening	– family audience, breakfast
Early morning drive-time	car drivers, home audience
Mid-morning audience	factories and home audience
Lunchtime audience	office staff on lunch break
Afternoon audience	representatives, drivers
Evening rush hour	homeward bound commuters
Evening/night	teenagers

The ease of production of radio advertising and the lower production costs make radio an attractive medium when used in conjunction with other types. On a cost per thousand basis, radio offers a useful addition to television campaigns. The use of jingles and complete songs as the background to television visuals allows easy transfer to radio as reinforcement.

Purchasing radio time

With assistance from the radio station in production, writing of copy and recording, local radio has a distinct appeal to the local advertiser wishing to undertake a campaign. Radio offers rating packages designed to deliver a guaranteed number of impacts in relation to the demographic groups within a target area. As in the case of TVRs the radio rating represents 1% of the target audience and are normally purchased in the form of packages, containing 100 ratings, rotated throughout a period of seven days.

With the high variation in audience levels throughout the day, to ensure this target being met, radio advertisements need to be repeated at regular intervals – usually in a series of rolling sequences to add variety and prevent listener annoyance. Discounts are offered in relationship to special conditions being met.

8.10   Cinema Advertising

Offering identical advantages to television by way of impact, colour, movement and sound – together with a vastly larger visual image – the only disadvantage being in the continued reduction in audiences. Research into cinema audiences shows that the average age of patrons is between 15-24 years, with little spread outside this group. Recall of the advertising message and brand names is greater following exposure to cinema advertising, probably as a result of the lack of distraction during the screening. However, this does not compensate for the lower audience levels.

Advertising can be purchased at individual cinemas, through cinema chains throughout the UK, or by being combined as a package with popular films on national distribution.

Also on offer are the standard series of advertising 'shorts' requiring only the addition of an end-of-track sound overlay, inviting consumers to enjoy a visit to the 'African Queen

Tandoori Restaurant – opposite this cinema'. These gems of cinematic history form valuable social and historical archive materials, yet are still preserved in working order throughout many cinemas in the UK.

8.11 Posters

Every year without fail one of the 180 000 poster sites in the country is rented amidst the greatest secrecy, and given over to an appeal from a thwarted lover seeking the hand of a fair maiden in marriage. As the object of his desire passes by on the top deck of the Clapham omnibus, she sees, along with her fellow passengers, the message 'MARRY ME, MARY' on a 48-sheet poster measuring 3048 x 6097 mm. In this public display of affection we have proof positive of the benefits of poster advertising. First, the sheer size creates an impact; second, posters can be placed close to the point of purchase, and third, it is a long-term investment.

Posters offer the advertiser colour, impact and the use of individual copy. Disadvantages are the lack of time available to study the message, and the problems of vandalism and weathering on the poster. Any poster campaign will require a considerable time for development, although the computerisation of sites enables selectivity to be improved. Sites are normally selected for a minimum period of one month or an open-ended contract. Poster sites in public places, stations, waiting rooms, have the ability to pass on a longer message.

Posters are seen by many environmental groups as a blot on the landscape, creating discord in the environment. To counter this the poster industry have undertaken considerable efforts to improve the appearance of many sites, covering vacant properties, development and slum areas from view and surrounding them with landscaped gardens.

Fig. 8.5 *Sizes for UK Poster Sites*

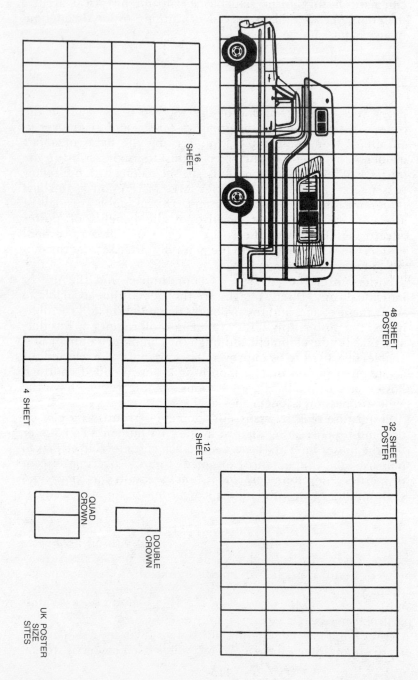

Chapter 9

Direct Marketing

Comments on the value of direct mail as a method of marketing are varied, both from those companies that use the medium, and individuals who receive the 'mail shots'. Individuals consistently report that they pay no attention to direct mail, referring to it as 'junk' and saying they consign it to the waste bin. The true figures reveal a different picture – less than one in every five mail shots is ignored.

Of the companies who utilise direct mail, many report that it forms a significant part of their marketing, consistently producing new customers and sales turnover. Research indicates that it is expanding faster than any other mass medium in the UK, with usage growing at a rate in excess of 20% each year.

9.1 What is Direct Mail?

Advertising is costed on the time or space used, while direct mail is normally composed of an individual cost for each shot, whatever the size of the contents. A mail shot can contain as many as eight sheets of information, together with pictures and samples of products.

Advertising does spread the sales message over a wide area of the market, but lacks the individual personal approach. Direct mail differs from advertising by being sent to a named individual in his or her own home, or place of business. This personalised approach offers a means of contacting specific market segments, and enables the sales message to be accurately focused on the particular needs of a person, family or company.

Requiring a lower minimum investment than any other form of promotion to be effective, it can , when used correctly, form the backbone of a company's promotional marketing. Direct mail still remains an under-utilised medium when measured by the number of separate users, and deserves consideration by any marketing executive.

Starting in direct mail

When utilised by the smaller company, direct mail can be carried out by using company secretarial staff to fold the sales literature, to insert it within the envelopes and to address, seal and post the finished envelope, Using your own staff allows considerable savings to be made over other media, and also provides direct control over the mail shot.

For the larger mailing, or where staff are unavailable, the work can be placed in the hands of a direct mail agency, who will carry out the same procedures, using automated filling and sealing. Their charges will add to the total cost of the operation, and must be taken into account when deciding the prices to charge for products on offer. If the total cost of the operation is £150 for each thousand letters sent out, and you receive orders from 4% of them, then you have spent £150 to gain 40 orders. To cover your costs each order must make your company a profit of at least £3.75. Ask yourself if this is possible before undertaking any direct mail promotion.

Direct mail lists

In order to send a personalised mail shot, you need a list of names and addresses to use. Normally two choices exist – to build or compile your own, or to rent a list from another company or list broker.

Any company will almost certainly have a list already, possibly fragmented, and almost certainly spread throughout the various departments. A list can soon be compiled from customers who are already buying, past customers who have moved to competitors, enquiries from prospective customers, and leads from advertising campaigns or sales representatives. To this list can be added names culled from directories, trade magazines, trade associations, *Yellow Pages*® – in fact from any suitable source. These names are your stock in trade for direct mail. They have the advantage of being currently in use, are specific to your market, and are of vital importance to any marketing promotion.

In retailing, the use of names and addresses for direct mail is often neglected, and yet they are easily obtained from guarantee cards, from delivery sheets, the back of cheques, licences, hire purchase applications, rentals, and credit agreements. If none of these are available as a source, then the organising of a simple raffle or prize draw, requiring customers to provide names and addresses, is often the simplest answer.

Bear in mind that a substantial list of current names and addresses can be rented to other non-competing business organisations in precisely the same way as others are willing to rent to you. The income resulting from this rental charge can assist in reducing the cost of compilation. Major national lists are offered through special direct mail list brokers, whose names can be obtained through the direct mail association. Brokers obtain their lists from a variety of sources. Magazines are willing to rent their subscription lists, trade and professional associations will supply lists of members, and many clubs, societies and groups rent the membership roll to brokers. A warning to those thinking in all innocence of subscribing to certain magazines – your name may well be rented to others without your knowledge, and the resultant flood of promotional offers can often cause considerable regret and embarrassment.

The normal rental agreement allows you to send one mailing shot to each address listed, and will usually be supplied in the form of computer-printed self-adhesive labels. Rental fees will vary according to accuracy and importance of the listing, but on average will fall between £40-£60 per thousand names. It is interesting that the list of residential addresses of 600+ millionaires in the UK attracts a higher rate – to prevent a flood of begging letters from poverty-stricken marketeers!

Any list supplied by a broker must be carefully checked to ensure that it has been compiled within the previous 18 months. Any list older than this will likely contain a high proportion of outdated and irrelevant details. A properly maintained list will have been checked to ensure that duplicate names do not appear, that each name has responded to previous mailings, and that errors have been removed. Computerisation of these lists allows the checking to be carried out automatically.

Brokers offer a wide range of listings, each profiled to ensure that promotional literature is sent to the correct type of individual or company. Lists can be profiled by occupation, interest, profession, or by area, postcode and district. The main point to bear in mind is that the list must represent people who are definitely interested in buying what you are offering. Remember that all written communications with customers, whether letters, delivery notes, invoices or parcels, can have direct mail promotion material included, so why waste the opportunity to send a direct mail promotion for little or no additional cost?

Creating the correct impression

Poor results from direct mail are the result of failing to create the right impression in the mind of the customer. A poor quality envelope, incorrectly addressed, containing badly printed litera-ture on cheap paper, can hardly improve customer confidence. So far as is possible within your budget, use the highest quality of material and production possible. A white envelope, bearing a postage stamp, with a typewritten address, will provide the most effective initial impression. Should budget or time constraints prevent this, then ensure the mail shot presents a clean, business-like appearance.

On no account address your mail to 'The Occupier', which shows a lack of interest and care, and is certain to result in the mail shot being ignored. Job titles should be used if available, and follow the personal name. Our personal name is important to us, and everyone expects to have it printed correctly. Careful main-tenance of the mailing list will include the checking of each letter returned by the Post Office as non-delivered. Removal of these names will ensure that the value of the list as a marketing tool is not destroyed.

The mail shot

Mail promotions will vary in content and style, ranging from a well-written letter telling the customer about your product or service, to a shot consisting of many different pieces of infor-mation. If we look carefully at the type of mail shot usually sent by larger direct mail users, such as the *Reader's Digest*, we will see that it usually consists of:

1   a personalised four-page letter, with gaps allowing the insertion of the prospect's name and address by computer;
2   a full-colour promotion leaflet, with photographs showing the product being used;
3   a certificate offering entry into a free draw for a prize – prizes are allocated by computerised random numbers and

the emphasis is on the customer returning the reply envelope to take part;

4   a special additional product, or bonus prize, for prospects returning the promotion reply within seven days;
5   a tear-off slip, requiring only the attachment of a self-adhesive stamp to reply;
6   two reply-paid envelopes for the return of the slip;
7   an order form offering the product on 14 days' trial.

The use of this type of mail shot has a proven success rate in gaining responses, and therefore deserves a closer look to see how this is achieved. The body of the letter is printed using a typestyle identical to that produced by a daisy-wheel typewriter/printer. The computer carrying the mailing list is programmed to insert various pieces of information at specified gaps in the text. In this way the letter is personalised by the inclusion of the town name, street name, number or customer name, at appropriate points.

Example

Dear *Mrs Thatcher*,

Your name has been included in our free one million pound prize draw, which could be yours to spend at any shop in *London*. Consider how easy it would be for your family to enjoy the holiday of a lifetime, or to add that new kitchen to *Downing St*. Perhaps you would prefer to use your prize in fitting double glazing to Number *10*. All these could be yours if you are successful in winning the main prize in our one million pound draw . . .

The example shown illustrates the sophisticated methods available to personalise the introductory letter and envelope. Direct mail agencies will undertake this type of operation, but the cost can prove high. Smaller companies using a lesser number of mail shots are able to add the name and greeting by typewriter or hand. This does of course require a considerable amount of time and effort, but the required effect is achieved. The greeting can also be printed in a casual typestyle, usually in blue ink, in an attempt to personalise.

Example

Dear Subscriber,

The use of a full-colour promotion leaflet is a normal method of marketing through direct mail. The copy should clearly explain the benefits to the customer and illustrate this by photographs showing the product in actual use.

Competitions are a popular promotion in mail shots, intended to encourage the customer to reply promptly. The advantage is that however many replies are received, the prize can only be won by one person, which enables the budget to be allocated accurately. There is never any chance of over-subscribing, as in a premium redemption scheme, and customers will not be disappointed, as all stand an equal chance of winning. Users of direct mail will often offer a bonus in the form of a free gift or increased prize to encourage a reply, as they are well aware that if the offer is not taken up within three or four days then the mail shot will be completely forgotten.

Prospects are not prepared to spend time looking for a pen, writing their names and addresses, finding a suitable envelope, buying a postage stamp and finally posting the reply. To encourage a reply, a tear-off strip or card should be enclosed with the literature. It is vital that the reply system is as easy to use as possible, and to encourage completion the slip should have as much information already printed by the sender as possible. The perfect reply slip should merely need ticks or self-adhesive stamps to be attached. Note that the name and address of the prospect can be inserted by computer. The smaller company without access to a computer may wish to invest in an addressograph machine which uses a series of individual stencils to address both envelope and reply slip.

The provision of a 'Freepost' reply address is an essential requirement of a direct mail operation, or, indeed, of any marketing scheme where a customer is expected to reply. 'Freepost' means free postage to the person sending the reply. The company or organisation who receive the envelope or card pay normal postage charges, plus a service fee. The business reply envelope or card has a pre-printed design for second or first class postage, and operates in a similar way to the 'Freepost' system, but is less versatile in methods of use. Further information on all the services offered can be found in the current issue of the *Post Office Guide*, obtainable from main Post Offices throughout the country.

By offering the customer the use of a product on trial for a period of time, marketing is relying on the inherent idleness of the customer. We are all the same. Once we have used a product for a length of time we become convinced of its value, and are then reluctant to return goods for a refund.

The sales letter

A sales letter is the written form of the selling conversation between a customer and the salesperson, and must follow the same rules.

In selling we use the mnemonic AIDA,

> *A*ttention
> *I*nterest
> *D*esire
> *A*ction

to summarise the correct method to use in selling a product. Your sales letter should follow the same sequence, and guide the customer through the benefits of your offer in a structured way, to finish with a call for definite action by 'replying today'.

Try to write your sales letter so that the prospective customer is always addressed as 'You'. Customers are not interested in your business problems or successes. What a customer wants to know from your letter is what your product will do for them. The impact of the sales letter lies in the way the information and benefits are expressed as facts which will appeal to the customer.

We start our sales letter by following the greeting with a headline question, which automatically makes the customer consider the answer in his or her mind. Examples could include:

'Do you want to save 50% on your telephone charges?'
'Have you at least six inches of insulation in your loft?'

Having gained the prospective customer's attention by informing him or her of the need for your product, we now move to the raising of the prospect's interest.

To write good copy for a direct mail, or sales letter, imagine the prospect is sitting opposite while you are reading the letter to him. Consider what would convince them of the benefits of your proposal and use words which will gain their interest. Describe the product in terms which would appeal to as many of their needs as possible. Does your product or service offer security – if so, then mention the free trial period or the money back guarantee. Status has an appeal to many customers, so stress the exclusivity of the product. Friendship is a powerful reason for many purchases – emphasise how many other customers have benefited from your service.

Marketing executives in advertising and direct mail are paid for writing copy that sells. You can learn from their experience by carefully reading all direct mail letters and advertising copy you see. They are aware that certain words paint a picture in the mind of the customer, and have a greater impact on the number of replies received during the campaign. If you wish to see examples of good copywriting, pay a visit to a nearby steakhouse and simply read the menu:

> Succulent Scotch beef steak, grilled to perfection over glowing pieces of charcoal, and served with a selection of freshly picked garden peas, young tender French beans and French fried potatoes. Ask for our special "barbecue" flavour dressing to complement your meal.

Is this not a more persuasive piece of copywriting than the local transport cafe's description of the same meal?

> Steak, two veg., with chips and gravy.

Good copywriting for direct mail will only come with considerable practice. When a letter or promotion shot has been used in several campaigns, there is always a strong temptation to alter the style, to discover if a rewrite will produce more replies. Provided a shot continues to bring in results, then retain the style and do not consider a change. Companies in direct mail for many years have discovered that once a shot is working, then it is foolish to change.

Having gained the customer's attention, aroused their interest, and built the desire to possess the product, we quite simply have to tell them what to do next. The most impressive piece of copy will have no effect if the customer has no idea how to place the order. We almost need to shout our demand for action at the customer. Weak endings give poor sales, and closing with 'We look forward to receiving your order' will never stir a customer to action. The closing paragraphs must encourage the prospect to reply, by offering one final benefit:

'Reply within 14 days for your free address book and directory.'
'Send today for your free desk clock, with your first order.'
'Post your subscription today, and enjoy three months' free trial.'

Each of these offers is designed to ensure the prospect replies promptly, as any delay means that the customer is almost bound to forget. All reply slips should be coded in some form or other to show the date dispatched, and/or the mailing list being used. This information, when collated, will give an indication of which particular day of dispatch produced the most replies.

When replies are received, marketing must ensure that the goods, information, catalogues or brochures are dispatched promptly. In cases where customers have forwarded cash or payment with the order, this prevents undue anxiety on the part of the sender. A standard acknowledgment can be forwarded if delay is likely. The prospect is then aware of this possibility, and is less likely to complain.

First-time users of direct mail should contact the local Post Office representative for details of the special offers and rebates available to both first-time users and those with high annual postings. The Post Office will also supply a number of free booklets on the use of direct mail in business marketing.

9.2 Communication

Every opportunity should be taken for improving communication with customers, both by sales staff and, more importantly, by use of the written word. Many companies have discovered how useful a newsletter can prove to be in keeping contact with clients. It enables the company to organise regular promotions for specific customers, to impart information, to provide advance warning of price or product alterations, and to build on the client-supplier relationship.

Although many newsletters or company magazines are produced by public relations consultancies, it is well within the capability of any alert marketeer to develop and sustain a simple six- or eight-page newsletter. The newsletter should always be sent on a regular basis – monthly, half-yearly – to build up the client expectation, rather than a heavyweight brochure at infrequent intervals. Simple line drawings of new products, together with descriptions and prices, special offers and information on products and company staff, all help to bind the customer to the supplier.

These can be inserted with all monthly statements of account, or in all delivery parcels. Order forms should be enclosed with the newsletter to encourage responses, an example being shown in Fig. 9.1.

As with all aspects of marketing, the use of one single medium by an organisation or company can cause too much reliance on continued orders from the same type of customer. We must ensure that the use of direct mail does not become an annoyance to customers by being over-used.

Fig. 9.1   *Example of Mail Shot Order Form*

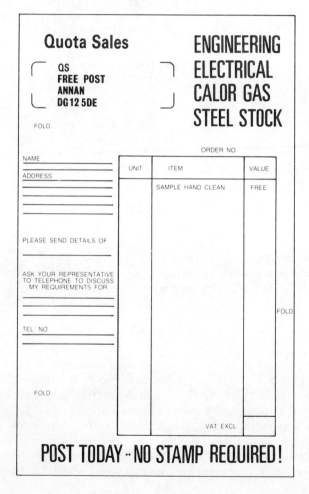

9.3   Leaflet Campaigns

In many ways leaflets are related to direct mail, in that this type of advertising medium is delivered more commonly to the customer's home. Leaflets are not as personal or specific as a direct mail shot. They are a general medium intended to saturate a market area around a business.

In fact most leaflets are so badly produced that they have little chance of impressing the customer. Crudely printed on inexpensive paper, they are scattered through letter-boxes with no effort to determine if the method is suitable for the type of product on offer.

A well-produced leaflet should conform to the direct mail 'AIDA' formula – Attention, Interest, Desire, Action – to maximise response. The leaflet should contain some type of offer which needs a response from the customer. The use of vouchers as part of the leaflet encourages reply, and can even be used as a free gift voucher when a representative makes a follow-up call.

Ensure that the leaflet is printed on both sides with copy and information. If not printed, then the leaflet is frequently used as a free scribbling sheet by the recipients. If factual information can be included on the leaflet, which would prove useful to the customer, then there is a strong possibility that the leaflet will be retained for future use by the customer.

Leaflet 'drops' are useful as an introduction to a new service or company in the area, and can be followed up by a personal call by the sales representative or management. Collate the results from leaflets returned or enquiries received, and try ringing the changes by delivering on different days, at different times, etc. Leaflets will always produce a lower response rate than direct mail, but have the advantage of being less expensive and useful in obtaining wide publicity and awareness for a company.

Fig. 9.2 shows a typical leaflet design, suitable for delivery over a sales area. Note the amount of black print used and the amount of copy included. Research shows that the greater the area of black, the more the leaflet is noticed. Once again, leaflets should be coded by the date of use, and a specific code for the area in which they have been delivered. All replies can then be quantified to discover the most effective day for responses.

9.4   Publicity and Public Relations

Public relations is additional to the role of advertising, where the image of a company or product is enhanced through an

Fig. 9.2 *A Promotion Leaflet*

organised series of events or campaigns. Public relations is best used in a positive sense, but can often be used in a negative environment. A company can suffer from a dramatic newsworthy event where public opinion turns rapidly against a product or service. Public relations will attempt to redress the balance by publicising and promoting the more positive aspects of the company and product.

Publicity is the promotion of a product by making it newsworthy. Publicity can be obtained by the endorsement of a product by a famous person, or a news story concerning an aspect of the company life. While this can sometimes be a fortunate accident, the marketing department of a company will ensure that the press are kept fully aware through correctly written news stories. This requires a specific range of journalistic skills, obtained through the services of a publicity consultancy, or through a company's own publicity department. This is sometimes classed as 'free advertising', but does involve companies in considerable staff expenses.

Publicity offers the opportunity to dramatise aspects of the corporate image or enhance the visibility of a product, with the added benefit that products gain prominence by appearing to be an item of news rather than advertising.

Advertising achieves results by being specific and timed for maximum effect. But publicity, dependent as it is on the whim of the media, is not so readily focused. Publicity is more useful in the broader function of building or sustaining corporate image.

The role of a public relations consultancy is to undertake the total promotion of an organisation or company to all those companies, consumers, public bodies and staff with which it is involved. All too often, companies fail to recognise that promoting the image of a company to customers and official bodies is not sufficient. Equal attention is needed to promote the company to its own staff. A true public relations consultancy will examine the total communication needs of a company and take steps to ensure maximum effect.

Public relations consultancies in the UK number around 600 and tend to specialise in certain areas. Some carry out work exclusively with public bodies, others with large multinationals, while some specialise in financial institutions. There are many individual public relations consultants who undertake consultancy duties on behalf of a limited number of small clients, almost on a self-employed basis.

In each case they act as outside consultants conducting the public relations function for a fee, as, unlike an advertising agency, they receive no commission for services supplied to clients. All the expenses and overheads must be charged to the client, usually by means of an agreed hourly rate. Thus all the duties carried out by a public relations consultancy are 'charged' out on the time taken. The range of tasks undertaken by consultancies varies with the client company, but can be summarised in general as:

- disseminating information;
- liaison duties;
- press relations;
- publicity and handling media enquiries.

Let us examine in more detail the various responsibilities under each of these headings.

9.5 Disseminating Information

PR undertakes the dissemination of information concerning company products or services, to the consumer, the media and to educational or special interest groups. The preparation of press releases, educational literature and general information is a highly skilled undertaking, requiring journalistic skills of a high order. The origination of press releases is discussed later in this chapter, together with practice exercises.

9.6 Liaison Duties

PR consultancies are engaged to liaise between a company and a number of official and semi-official centres of opinion throughout the country. They will act as parliamentary lobbyists, approaching Members of the Commons and House of Lords, to represent the client's point of view on issues of importance. Consultation with Members of Parliament will provide information of forthcoming papers, bills and legislation likely to affect their clients.

In many companies they undertake liaison between the management and members of staff, often being involved in the presentation of company objectives, by means of seminars and short 'one off' events. This can often be extended further into liaison between a client company and their sales force or distributors. These can be in the form of formal presentations to the work force of forthcoming developments, the editing of staff magazines, company and dealer information newsletters, or the arrangement of factory open days for dealers, public and staff.

9.7 Sponsorship

Sponsorship in particular is an increasing area of PR requiring considerable liaison between the company and those they wish to sponsor, to ensure that the maximum benefit is gained. Consultancies are responsible for the arranging of suitable sponsorship, publicity and subsequent merchandising.

We see these developments in the increasing use of sponsorship within the sports field. Recent developments are the sponsorship of the Football League by a number of companies, Cricket League sponsorship, and in the field of motor racing. The real significance of some of this sponsorship lies not so much in the publicity or public relations benefit, but rather in the opportunity for 'free' coverage on the TV channels, both in the UK and worldwide. Each sight of a company logo, or mention of a product name, represents an adequate return on the sponsorship. Most sponsorship is often conducted at lower levels, far removed from national publicity, possibly in the purchase of new kit for local teams, the association of a company name with local events, or in the 'semi-charitable' work carried out.

9.8 Press Relations

The importance of the press in public relations is best illustrated by noting the growth of published media in the UK. Despite the advantages of TV with the ability to give an instant picture of happenings anywhere in the world, the number of readers taking newspapers, magazines and other forms of printed material far exceeds the number of viewers tuning into any particular programme.

The total spoken content of an average televised news programme would be insufficient to fill the front page of the average daily paper, or a single page of a typical magazine. The press provides coverage in depth of any event, with specialised sections for items of importance, ensuring coverage of the most unusual product.

No consultancy or company can expect to utilise the press to give only favourable publicity. Total control of the press in a free society is impossible, and should not be expected. By seeking to publicise a product, or gain mentions favourable to a company, the public relations consultancy may find that they have unleashed a double-edged weapon. A consultancy or company placing itself in the public eye will automatically be expected to account to the press for both favourable and unfavourable events. The task of the public relations consultancy is to deal with both in a similar manner, dealing fairly with the press in all areas. Should an occasion arise where the reporters seek an interview on a difficult subject, the spokesperson should speak with honesty and conviction, and not seek to hide the true facts. However unpalatable the subject, never take refuge in the use of 'no comment', which only causes resentment. Should the event be one where full information is not yet available, a decision has yet to be made, or is confined to legal proceedings, this should be explained to the press and their co-operation sought.

9.9   Publicity and Handling Media Enquiries

Composing a press release

A press release is the most common method of informing an editor about a company. Many continue to be badly composed and written, and thus face rejection by the press.

Reporters and editors are in business to sell newspapers, and not to provide a sounding-board for the company. Press relations are not propaganda, and if used must be at all times in the form of credible information. A company may consider a recent large order to be of world-shaking significance, but to the editor and public it is of little importance when compared with major world events. To receive editorial mention the story must be of current interest and value. Far too few company management bother to carefully read the daily press and isolate the stories which may have a relevance to their products. A well-timed press release related to a current story, giving further information or providing a comment, is more likely to receive editorial space than an item unrelated to events.

The press are not prepared to publish as news, releases which could be considered as free advertising. They are quite capable of seeing through a story to the basic advertising message being offered. Therefore, when preparing a press release, it is important to follow certain guidelines.

1   Type in double line spacing on a single sheet of A4 white paper.
2   Include a heading giving a brief indication of the contents of the release.
3   Leave ample left- and right-hand margins.

4   Write in the third person. Do not use the pronouns you, we or us.

5   When appropriate to the story, and to add interest, use verbal remarks which should be surrounded by quotations – 'We are delighted by the response to our special offers,' said marketing manager Mr Richard Watson.

6   At the end of the press release, give the name of a suitable company contact together with a telephone number.

7   Count the number of words in the press release and note this at bottom of the final page. This helps the editors to determine the space required, and may help your release to be published as a quick 'space filler'.

8   Ensure that facts quoted in the press release are accurate.

9   Mark press release for date of publication (known as an embargo) to prevent the story being published before the event has taken place, or where prior publication would be unwise. Most editors will respect this request.

10 The length of a press release should not normally be greater than 200-300 words.

A good release will answer the following queries:

- *What* is the subject of the story?
- *Where* is the story taking place?
- *Who* is the story about?
- *When* is the event taking place?
- *How* will it happen?

A press release must be written in a way that will match the style of the publication to which it is sent. We must bear in mind that modern newspapers prefer a short, snappy reporting style rather than long-winded paragraphs.

The best way of refining the writing of a press release is to institute a programme of sending a selected number of journals items of interest, on a regular basis. This will quickly reveal the most effective type of release, simply by noting those which are published and those which are not. Remember that local journalists and newspapers are more likely to use press releases which have a local flavour or interest, but on the other hand it is useless sending a national paper items of minor significance. Correct selection of the recipient is vital to ensure publication.

9.10   Press Conferences

These usually occur as the result of events outside the company, requiring the management to pass on information to a large number of media reporters. Often called at short notice, either in the company plant or local hotels, they are an opportunity for the media to receive a statement from the company or person concerned, and to ask questions to clarify the story. On occasions such as this, there is even greater need for a trained public relations consultant to be present during the conference.

Press conferences prevent the scramble for comments which occurs when an important story breaks. Without a conference there is a strong possibility that comments will be sought from members of the company who are inexperienced in handling the press, and the resulting statements and editorial comment will not fairly reflect the full picture.

9.11   Press Receptions

To publicise an important company event, public relations consultants will organise a press reception, inviting selected journalists, reporters and feature writers to attend. These events need careful organisation to be effective. The media receive many invitations to press receptions, and tend to be highly selective in those they choose to attend.

The invitation should clearly indicate the purpose of the reception, and preferably be located in an easily accessible venue. Transport is often provided, together with suitable refreshments. The reception will consist of a series of presentations, based around the product or event. Arrangements should be made for those attending to sample, question, or to learn more of the background. Those holding the press reception will supply press packs, giving factual information, photographs and comprehensive information.

9.12   Press Photographs

In the words of the old Chinese saying, 'A picture speaks a thousand words', so an interesting and informative photograph will provide extra impetus to any news release or event. No self-respecting journal or paper will be prepared to publish photographs better suited to the average photo album. Use professional photographers, or leave well alone.

In general the print should be not less than 10 x 8 inches in size, either black and white, or colour suitable for colour separation. A clear caption giving details of the photograph should be attached to the back of the print. The names of any persons shown in the photographs are written from left to right, and from front to back. During press receptions and other events the public relations consultant will ensure that photo opportunities are provided, with a full range of products on show or in use, and personalities on hand.

Assignment

Your task is to pick an aspect of your business, college course, hobby or interest and produce a press release suitable for publication in your local weekly paper. The press release should be a minimum length of 200 words, and follow all the points made in the preceding chapter. The example below can be utilised as the basis for your press release. The press release should be typewritten or produced by word processor, and be fully capable of being distributed to suitable media.

Fig. 9.3 *Sample Press Release*

Chapter 10

International Marketing

As an offshore race we tend to be somewhat insular in our outlook, and while not refusing the opportunities available through export, we tend to see exporting as primarily the responsibility of the larger organisation or company with an exporting/marketing department.

Despite the high costs, estimated to be in excess of £100 000, involved in setting up a new department within a company to carry out exporting, it does offer a number of advantages. All companies seek to increase their markets or sales turnover, and many have discovered the relative ease with which a strong home brand can be marketed throughout the world. There is, of course, more to exporting than a salesperson simply grabbing their executive briefcase, a convenient flight, and arriving unannounced in some foreign country, expecting to sell to the local market. Not since the Red Indians sold Manhattan for strings of beads has that been the case!

10.1 Reasons for Exporting

Export marketing needs to be just as carefully analysed and investigated as is the home market. Reasons for entering the export market are many, but in general will fall into one of the following major categories.

Extension of product life-cycle

In the Western industrial nations we rely greatly on sophisticated technology to assist with and control our lives. In undeveloped economies the need for this level of technology is less, and products which have reached the end of their Western life-cycle or are operating in a highly competitive market can have considerable export potential.

Example

The potential for error in export marketing was the provision to Indian villages of small petrol-operated water pumps intended to provide a fresh supply from deep wells, during drought or contamination by disease. Despite the simplicity of the power source to Western eyes, the provision of new spark plugs presented an insurmountable problem when the time came to service the pump. Far more effective would have been to supply simple hand pumps with the capability of being easily repaired using technology available in the village.

Companies must look at the product range on offer in their home market and consider if the technology being used would allow the product to meet the needs of the less developed market. It may be possible to license the product to a local company for production completely within the ethnic market, or to supply parts for assembly by the local labour force.

Improvement in the product profitability

Through a combination of circumstances the profitability of many products is greater in the export market than may be the case in the home market. Reasons for this can vary, but could often be that the foreignness of the product is thought to add a touch of exclusivity or chic, resulting in a premium price being obtained. A prime market for Scotch whisky is Japan, with the product having a cachet of luxury and status, and attracting premium prices over the home-based Suntory whisky. Despite the efforts of the Japan-based distillers, and a price which is the equivalent of a whole day's salary, the Tokyo businessman will not abstain from his genuine glass of Scotch.

Financial considerations

The potential financial benefit which comes from involvement in exporting is in the raising of finance and in the reduction of taxation. Taxation benefits for exporters setting up manufacturing plants within foreign host countries, together with the ability to switch profits between countries, enables taxation to be reduced to a considerably lower rate than would be the case with a purely home-based market. The availability of government investment, of advantageous loan rates, and of foreign sources of capital is increased in the export market.

Spreading the risk of a market downturn

The more international the areas within which a company markets, the less the risk of a serious downturn in the market caused by political, economic or financial considerations. Business balance will almost certainly result in a reduction in sales in one market being compensated by a corresponding increase in another market. International companies will ensure strong representation in as many markets as possible.

New product development

Export markets are fertile ground for the development of new products or variations of the existing range. Product testing under different conditions will often produce a worthwhile modification, which can then be offered to other markets.

Balance of payments

The number of government schemes intended to assist in the promotion of products in foreign markets clearly illustrates the importance in balancing imports by a corresponding amount of exports. Her Majesty has instituted the Queen's Award for Export Achievement as a tangible sign of improved export performance. The international trading and standing of a company is assisted by having a presence in the major markets of the world. This produces greater awareness of the company and the products in the eye of the potential customer and shareholder.

10.2   Marketing Overseas

In general the methods of marketing products or services

overseas follow the same sequence as in the home market:

1 research into the market;
2 research into the product;
3 research into customers;
4 identification of key markets;
5 product design and packaging;
6 test marketing;
7 decisions on selling methods;
8 appointing a distributor;
9 advertising and sales promotion;
10 after-sales service and repair.

Fuller general information on each of these areas will be found in the preceding sections. This section covers the important differences between home and export marketing. International marketing is strewn with traps which can so easily catch the marketeer.

Research into the market

For the smaller company first seeking to enter an export market, the possibility of undertaking actual market research in the target country would be a very expensive proposition, and unlikely to produce cost effective results. Potential exporters will be forced to utilise existing market information sources, which will be obtained from a number of sources.

The major source of information on potential export markets is through the government-sponsored British Overseas Trade Board or BOTB, who prepare and distribute market reports and export opportunities on a monthly basis for a small charge. The BOTB will prepare a more detailed report on export markets for a nominal fee, which can identify many of the problems most likely to occur. Customs and Excise maintain data on imports into the UK, which can form a source of market-potential information for original equipment suppliers or raw material providers. UK clearing banks are pleased to help not only in the financial aspects of exportation, but also through the provision of limited market reports through their overseas branches.

The value of the information obtained can of course vary, dependent on the quality of the staff employed in the local branch of the export country. All banks would be happy to assist in the provision of information even though the company requesting may not be a customer. They expect by assisting to gain more business. Major market research organisations can provide market information on a worldwide basis, together with information available from the commercial attachés of the British embassies throughout the world.

Research into the product

Export marketing is full of stories of products which failed, caused misunderstandings with customers, or even, in some cases, caused injury through incorrect usage.

Example

Serious problems occurred with dried milk for babies, used by new mothers in the underdeveloped countries of Africa. The advertising of baby milk consisted of billboards showing healthy, happy, rotund, almost overweight little infants gurgling contentedly on a baby-feeding bottle containing dried milk feed.

Some mothers proved unable to understand clearly the mixing and measurements used in preparing feeds. They assumed that a single measure of milk produced instant healthy little offspring – and in view of the expense of the product many mothers made the decision that if one spoon produced such outstanding results – then half a spoon would have some effect although perhaps a little one, on the child's development. We then had the situation developing where children were actually suffering malnutrition through being fed on a short measure of what was essentially a correctly balanced infant food product.

Through poor product design and research, coupled with both incorrect advertising and instructions for the market segment and type of customer, the World Health Organisation was forced to intervene to prevent further misuse.

What does this tell us about export marketing? It shows how difficult is the task of ensuring that the product design, instructions, branding and colours meet the needs of the population and market. The way in which the population of a country or market visualise a product is formed, not just from their particular environment, but also in the way that certain reference factors influence behaviour and perception.

Marketing management must be aware of the way in which everyone throughout the world tends to assume that their preferences, needs and habits are the 'proper' way of behaving. This leads the home market to consider that the 'foreign' method of operating is wrong or incorrect. How many times have we heard ourselves, or others, say while on holiday, 'I don't like the way in which these people behave at dinner . . .'

These factors clash most when related to the eating habits, etiquette, toilet habits and sexual behaviour of the population in question. Cultural taboos are of importance to all societies, including our own, where certain products or colours can cause offence, if used incorrectly in the packaging, advertising or sales promotion. Examples are many, but include:

> white is the colour of mourning in Japan;
> Latin America considers purple the colour of death;
> pairs of items are disapproved of in Ghana.

Marketing must seek local advice, or advice from BOTB or the commercial attaché in the relevant country before attempting to market a new product.

Research into customers

Research into segmenting the market by customer needs requires information on the various factors influencing the decision to purchase. In the case of the consumer market this is classified into several areas. Chief amongst these are religious, cultural and ethnic considerations; family background, per capita income, expectations, health, housing, services, education, class structure and product usage.

Different considerations will influence industrial buyers. They will base decisions on:

- the level of prevailing technology;
- degree of industrialisation and standardisation;
- availability of skilled personnel and training facility;
- state of the economy and exchange rates;
- political stability;
- health and safety considerations;
- legal and trade union restrictions.

Identification of key markets

Some companies achieve exports but others, as the saying goes, have exports thrust upon them. Smaller companies tend to find they are approached to export in a number of different ways: by buyers arriving from abroad at the factory with little more than an address on a slip of paper, or by fully-fledged inward-buying missions sponsored by chambers of commerce or trade interest groups.

A brand can spread from the home market personal export, where individual visitors, often tourists, purchase products for their own use. Thus companies may find that approaches are made by buying offices, based in the UK, on behalf of foreign retailers. Demand in the export market based on the personal exports has often prompted an approach for direct supplies. Confirming houses carry out a similar task on behalf of larger buyers, acting on behalf of governments or larger state enterprises. They purchase products in the UK, arrange transportation and, more importantly, arrange for payment to be made.

This rather haphazard approach to export marketing does allow easy entry into the export markets, with the possibility that sales will expand. However, acting through any third party organisation means that the manufacturer seeking to export is very much at the mercy of a sudden change in supplier.

Far more effective is to identify those key markets which would be best suited to the present marketing style of the company. Each company will have particular products or services which will have a potential overseas key market, that is, ones that are similar in most aspects to the home market. This similarity is mostly by culture, background, stage of development, ease of access both by transport and import controls, and a shared common language. Because of this common ground the produce needs little alteration to be accepted by the market.

There is a tale, supposedly true, of two export sales staff who arrived in a foreign market to sell their company range of shoes. One telexed the company with the message: 'No demand for product – no-one has ever worn shoes – all barefoot – returning home next flight.'

The other telexed: 'Send extra samples – huge market opportunity – all barefoot – urgently need shoes.'

A perspective on the same market from differing points of view.

Is your company market follower or market leader?

Product design and packaging

Product formulation and design are similar to the existing home market, but with the following additional provisions:

1 the product should conform with an individual country's laws concerning labelling, safety markings and standards;
2 instructions should be easy to understand, relying heavily on graphic illustrations rather than writing;
3 care should be taken over design of logo, product shape, colour and naming of product.

Specialist advice is again required on these areas, available from BOTB. Packing should be suitable for the journey and eventual storage of the product and to ensure arrival in acceptable condition.

Test marketing

Provided the required research has been carried out into the possible demand for the product or service on offer in the export market, then limited test marketing can be arranged.

The 'halo' effect, where a product has reached such a stage of development or marketing that it is almost impossible to stop, can have an enhanced impact in an export market. Often caused by the natural wish of export agents to encourage the entry of a new product into the market, they tend to exaggerate the possible sales potential of a product.

Provided accurate opinions on a product can be obtained, it is wise to ask manufacturers, retailers or consumers to undertake a test market of the product over as wide a spread of the potential market as possible. Treat the results with care, discover the true results of the test and, if possible, isolate the factors which influenced the purchase so that subsequent sales promotion or advertising can be effective.

Decision on selling methods

Selling in the export market-place should be seen as being in two separate parts. The first part is the sales organisation, set up at the home base to support the sales effort overseas. The second part is the type of organisational structure best able to serve the company in the actual export market. Sales are carried out either direct to the ultimate user, or indirectly through a distributor, each offering distinct advantages and disadvantages to the exporter.

An export sales office must possess all the features of a home sales office plus familiarity with the languages and customs of relevant countries. Fluency in spoken and written French, Spanish or German is essential, and will cover communication in most markets. The ability to speak Japanese or Chinese is an invaluable additional skill, and, it should be noted, already forms part of the course in colleges and schools in New Zealand and Australia. Although specialised translation services are available through most chambers of commerce, they cannot compensate for a lack of bilingual staff in the UK sales office. Communication facilities such as fax machines should be available, together with photocopying facilities, as a response to the considerable amount of extra paperwork generated by export sales.

Appointing a distributor

Distributors act on behalf of an exporter, and are usually nationals of the country concerned, with a considerable understanding of the customs and requirements of the particular market in which they operate. These are usually major multiple-product distributors acting for several UK manufacturers and companies, and we must ask the following questions before offering an appointment:

1   What type of company is the distributor?
2   Does it offer general products, or is it specific to our market?
3   Do they have specialist knowledge of the market for our product in their country?
4   What range of products does the distributor handle?
5   Does the distributor handle any products from our competitors or their subsidiaries?
6   Where is the distributor located?
7   Are they near to ports, centres of population or markets?
8   How long has the company been in operation?
9   What is their credit rating?
10   What opinion of the distributor is held by other respected businesses in the community?

11 Do the personnel of the company have knowledge of the market, and can they be trained further?

12 Does the company have experience of importing as well as sales marketing?

13 Can they undertake promotion work handling exhibitions, local advertising, etc.?

14 Do you consider they would be capable of working with your company on a long-term basis?

While the ideal distributor is almost impossible to find, we use this checklist to identify the particular strengths and weaknesses of the distributor we are seeking to appoint. We must then try, through comprehensive training and support, to improve the skills of the distributor.

Advertising and sales promotion

We would have no problem in advertising our products world-wide, if everyone spoke and read the same language. But this is not so, and presents a problem to the overseas marketeer. Consider the number of occasions when examples of the comical use of English in menus, hotel brochures or instructions appear in the newspapers or on television. For example:

'Quite guest house with big widows. Running cot, and hold water.'

To maintain credibility, the export marketing executive will first employ the services of a professional translation agency to prepare body copy in the language and idiom of the country in question. To prove that the translation has been carried out correctly, pass on the translation to a further agency and request a translation back into English. This reveals any hidden flaws in the vernacular use of language.

Appointing an advertising agency

We have a number of choices in selecting which type of advertising agency would be most suitable for our marketing:

1. Use could be made of the current UK agency, which may have links, associations, or, indeed, be part of an international agency.

2. Employ an existing international agency, bearing in mind the minimum budget figure on advertising they would

require. Do we expect to achieve the type of budget figure in the particular export market we are concerned with?
3. Use an advertising agency based within the country where we are to market, and staffed by nationals. By using a national agency we will be able to ensure that our advertising is carried out in the most effective way, and that our distributors are closely involved and supportive.

To expect to control advertising carried out in an export market from the UK without the assistance of a local agency, or branch office of an international agency, is a recipe for wasted advertising expenditure. The following checklist is for use when considering the appointment of an export advertising agency, and has many features in common with that used when carrying out the same task in the UK.

Financial considerations

1   What method is to be used in deciding payment for services carried out by the agency? E.g. based on commission or costed on an 'as used' basis?
2   What is the total cost expected to be?

Client listing

1   Has the proposed agency previous experience of our product and market?
2   Are any of the agency's present clients our competitors in this market, or in others?

Staff and expertise

1   Is the agency able to effectively transfer our style of advertising and company image into their market?
2   Which personnel from the agency will be working in co-operation with ourselves and our appointed distributors?
3   Do they have sufficient knowledge of written and spoken English to be able to communicate effectively with members of our company?

Background

1   Does the agency have long experience of the market and the restrictions, legal constraints, religious and nationalistic ethics of the country?

2 Are communication methods between the agency and ourselves acceptable?

3 What proportion of their total billing does our budget represent?

4 Do we feel confident that the initial enthusiasm shown by the agency will continue?

5 Have we faith in the competence and professionalism of the agency?

After-sales service and repair

Products which are marketed internationally require a network of comprehensive after-sales and service facilities throughout the world. In many countries the purchase of a foreign product represents a major investment, or is the result of a long-term effort in completing documentation and obtaining authority to import. The purchasers, be they individuals, companies, state enterprises or governments, will demand considerable after-sales service. After-sales service for exported products is a greater commitment than in a home market, due mainly to the distance separating the manufacturing company and the importer. The following points will need to be carefully considered before deciding on what level of after-sales service to undertake:

Product service

1 Is the product, once installed, unlikely to be moved?

2 Do we therefore require on-site repair facilities and trained staff or technicians?

3 Are we able to train nationals in the country to carry out this task?

4 Do we need to have expatriate staff in control of this operation, bearing in mind the high costs involved?

5 Are spare parts of the required standard available in the importing country?

6 Are we able to supply and keep available stocks of replacement or consumable items within the importing country?

7 Would we have a problem over 'fake' replacement parts which could be offered to our customers?

8 How would the customer react to such an offer?

9 Do import duties and internal taxes make spare parts and replacements a high-cost item?

10 Do different conditions of use increase the risk of breakdown?

11 Can maintenance services be carried out, or will customers ignore checking correct operation?

12 Will this neglect invalidate any guarantees and warranties we may offer?

Installation

1 Are the serviceability and operation of our product dependent upon the supply of other services or supplies outside our control?

2 Do preconditions have to be met before our product can be properly installed or supplied?

3 What operator-training is required?

4 What likely effect would any damage during transportation have on the installation of the product?

5 Are instructions on installation or usage clear and unambiguous?

6 Are detailed listings given of all spare parts, together with order codes?

7 Does the client require a turnkey operation?

Capital equipment supplied for export will require a major investment in after-sales service. With consumer-type products the requirement is normally for service or replacement, and in this case it is sufficient to appoint an existing service organisation in the particular country to undertake this function with any defective product. Certain worldwide products, Pentax cameras, Philips Electrical, Braun shavers and roller brushes, for example, carry literature within the package giving the names and addresses of appointed service agents in countries throughout the world.

Emphasis in the promotional literature and company advertising concerning the efforts and stock-holding investment made by the company to ensure service, results in increased confidence in the product. This is one of the major factors which has to be overcome by any company exporting into a new market. Almost every customer investing in what, to them, is essentially a foreign product needs the reassurance that any problems with the product will be quickly remedied. This technique has been effectively used by Volvo cars, who emphasise the high content of UK-manufactured parts in their vehicles. The implied security which results from this is strongly featured in the advertising.

10.3   Invisible Earnings – The Service Industry

The UK is a rarity in the world export market in being a major exporter of services. The decline of manufacturing industry in the UK from the 1970s has resulted in increased reliance on service industry income. This results in a favourable balance to the economy of approximately 800 million pounds per month. Income is produced from the following categories of service:

- banking, insurance and finance;
- shipping;
- entertainment;
- air transport;
- construction;
- training.

Incoming tourism is a form of export service income, but is not calculated in the balance of payments figure.

As with all services the problem lies in making sure that standards are maintained, despite the difficulties each market and country presents to the company. A service can only be as good as the last time it was used. To be sure of success we need to have strict control over the operation and the training of local staff, which can prove difficult. The differing educational standards and background of these employees can prevent the image of the service concept being fully understood or implemented.

The turnover of service companies throughout the world is increasing as a result of certain factors.

(a)   Improved standards of living, and disposable income

As income increases, a greater amount is available for use in discretionary purchases, including travel and tourism, and individual investment in financial institutions.

(b)   Worldwide standardisation of service-type organisations

As multinational service organisations spread throughout countries, so different nationalities and cultures accept similar standards of service and product.

Example

The development of fast-food outlets, offering a range of standardised food packages served in standard surroundings has resulted in consumers expecting, and relying, upon an identical meal being served at any point in the world. Consumers enter any of the fast-food chains expecting their Wimpy or Big Mac to appear and taste the same as in their local outlet.

(c) The growth of the European Common Market and the reduction in tariff barriers and restrictions to trade

EEC efforts to reduce and standardise trade barriers have resulted in the development of service industries which can operate through a number of countries, secure in the knowledge that competition is not prevented by high trade barriers.

(d) Changes in the population age groups resulting from improved health care and life expectancy

The population of the developed countries is altering significantly through improved health care facilities giving longer life expectancy. This then results in greater demands for leisure industries, service facilities, caring services, and yet again the provision of finance and investment service.

(e) Alterations in consumer expectations, from ownership to rental

Aggressive marketing by service industries has resulted in a trend away from ownership, towards the use of consumer products on a rental or time-sharing basis.

The student of marketing, or expanding business management, must consider carefully before deciding to ignore the advantages of exporting. While appearing to present difficulties in the initial stages of setting up, the advantages of a flourishing export market with its subsequent benefits in expanding the outlook of the company is worthwhile.

Assignment

You are the newly appointed marketing assistant to Deepwater Export plc, a company involved in the marketing of simple hand-operated water pumps. The product will lift a vertical head of water some eight metres, or pump water over a distance of 100 metres. The option exists for a simple conversion to powered pumping operation using any convenient motive source – human or animal power, internal combustion engine or wind power.

However, the main advantage lies in the ease of assembly from a number of simple parts, well within the constructional ability of any of the average population in underdeveloped countries. The pumping chamber is supplied ready assembled and all other parts are secured with the simple tools supplied to form a heavy-duty pumping station. Equipment can be fitted which will filter the supply to a standard approved by the World Health Organisation.

Your task as the marketing assistant is to:

1　Target a number of suitable key export markets with potential for sales of the new Deepwater Handipump V, and give reasons for your choice.
2　Detail the factors which you need to consider in deciding on a suitable selling method for the pump in your key markets.
3　Draft suitable copy for an advertisement to be placed in the largest-circulation newspaper of your key market countries.
4　Investigate the various sources of secondary market research information which would be available concerning one of the key market countries you have chosen.

The assignment should be in the form of a report to be sent to the marketing manager of Deepwater – Mr Harold Napton.

Chapter 11

Protecting the Consumer

In a complex marketing and production system, it is often difficult for consumers to be sure that the product they are purchasing meets all the standards they might reasonably expect. In this country successive governments have established guidelines for manufacturers, and enacted legislation to protect the consumer. The following sections deal with those which affect the marketeer.

11.1 Trade Descriptions Act 1968

Let us commence by examining the Act which concerns itself with the selling and marketing of products by way of trade. The Trade Descriptions Acts of 1968 and 1972 allow criminal action to be taken against business organisations only, and not the private seller. If the private buyer considers that the terms of a contract have been breached, they have a remedy only through the civil courts. However, when goods or services are supplied during the course of business or trade, the Act makes it an offence to:

- apply a false trade description to goods, or supply goods to which a false trade description has been applied;
- make a false statement knowingly or recklessly as to the provision of service, accommodation or facilities; or
- give a false indication as to price.

A trade description can be any information provided with a product, or with the advertising, relating to the quantity, size, method of production, date or place of manufacture, country of origin, size, contents, testing or approval, history, including any previous ownership or use, etc. It also covers any verbal description applied by the seller, or buyer, to a product.

This all-embracing area demands attention by the marketing and advertising department of all companies and agencies to ensure that all statements concerning a product are accurate. However, to be false the description must clearly affect the consumer's perception of the product. Typical trade puffery such as 'new', 'beautiful' or 'spectacular' are not seen as being false trade descriptions, but any description related to a quality or attribute must be accurate.

Many salespersons wrongly believe that verbal descriptions supplied by them during a sales interview are not covered by the Trade Descriptions Act. Of equal importance, and often disregarded, is any trade description applied to the product by the customer – 'Is this dress real silk?' is covered by the Act, so ensure that your answer is correct. Provided that the description you give is based on information supplied by the manufacturer, the liability rests with the supplier for false descriptions.

11.2 Powers of the Office of Fair Trading

The Director General can decide from information received that a company's actions are detrimental to the interests of the consumer. A formal request is made to the company, asking for a clear promise that the action will stop. If a trader refuses to give that promise, then the Director General has the power to take the trader before the Restrictive Practices Court. A breach of an order made by the Court is a serious offence which can result in penalties and an injunction to cease trading.

11.3 Trade Descriptions Act 1972

The main purpose of this additional legislation is to stop foreign-made goods being sold as originating in the UK. No offence is committed if the supplier can show that:

- the mark or name of the country of origin is present on the goods, even if inconspicuous;
- the seller could not possibly have known that the goods were foreign-made;
- the seller did not have any reason to know that the mark or name was not of UK origin.

Trade descriptions in service industries

The supplying of a false description 'recklessly or knowingly' in relation to services or accommodation is difficult to prove, but in general the tour operator/supplier of any service should ensure by checking as far as possible the correctness of statements made in the brochure. It would clearly be reckless if no attempt was made by a tour operator to check the description given by a hotel operator in a resort. The adherence by a supplier or manufacturer to a code of practice set by a suitable trade body, for example, the Association of British Travel Agents, or the Motor Agents' Association, will enable the members of such an association to show compliance with the spirit of the Act.

A code of practice is a voluntary statement made by an association or trade body, giving the level of service or business standards expected by their membership. Although these codes are not legally binding, they are a useful bench mark in determining whether a breach has occurred, and can be of value as evidence. The Director General of Fair Trading will encourage and approve the continued provision of these codes in furthering the cause of consumer protection.

Disclaimers

The use of a disclaimer to limit trade descriptions must be stated as clearly and boldly as the original. The most common example is found in the clause attached to details of properties offered for sale by estate agents, which reads:

> The vendors of the property give notice that these particulars, although believed to be correct do not constitute part of any offer or contract, that all statements in these particulars as to this property are made without responsibility and are not to be relied on as statements or representations of fact or warranty whatsoever in relation to this property. The intending purchaser must satisfy himself by inspection or otherwise as to the correctness of each of the statements contained in these particulars.

11.4   False Indications of Price

With the abolition of recommended retail prices in 1964, consumers were no longer able to make clear comparisons between 'before sale' and 'after sale' prices. In an attempt to resolve the number of false comparisons being made, legislation was brought before Parliament which evolved into the present Trade Descriptions Act. The subsequent legislation has itself caused a veritable flood of comparison prices, many of which prove to be contrived or false. The Trade Descriptions Act requires that before a comparison can be made between prices the higher price must have been charged for a minimum of 28 days during the previous six months. It would appear legally correct for some companies to meet these conditions in their Orkney branch, and use this higher price as a comparison for a sale in Oxford Street. Hardly a comparison in the spirit of consumer protection.

11.5 Unlawful Notices

The display of any notice stating 'no refunds' or 'no exchanges' could be interpreted as limiting a customer's rights under the Sale of Goods or Supply of Goods Act, and would be evidence of a criminal act. Any notice by a supplier concerning the obligations undertaken by a warranty or guarantee must also make it clear that the customer's rights are not reduced. Bear in mind that the customer's statutory rights are not affected by the price charged for the goods or services, even goods sold in a sale situation, so disclaimer notices stating 'no exchange or refund on sales goods' are not permitted.

11.6 The Consumer Safety Act 1978

As in the Health and Safety at Work Act, the Consumer Safety Act is an enabling Act, allowing the Secretary of State to make provision for consumer safety. Any product which is potentially dangerous can be prohibited from being sold, or a notice can be issued warning of the danger.

Suppliers who disregard such a notice will find themselves committing a criminal offence, in addition to being sued in the civil court for damages. The existing British Safety Standards are, in many cases, used as the standard safety regulations. These standards cover such areas as heating by electricity and oil, kitchen appliances, children's clothing, etc.

Trading Standards officers are employed by local councils to ensure that the standards are complied with, and have been instrumental in ensuring that considerable publicity is given to foreign imports which do not meet UK standards. Any manufacturer or supplier must ensure that the products they offer, whether UK or imported, do meet with the required standards.

11.7   Consumer Protection Act 1987

The Consumer Protection Act 1987 gives rights to any person injured by a product. The manufacturer is strictly liable for any injury and the provisions also give the same protection for anyone injured by a defective product, even though they may not have purchased the item themselves.

This liability does not cover products purchased before March 1988, but for products supplied after that date the Act allows anyone who has been injured as a direct result of a faulty product to sue the producer or the importer. Liability is joint and several, which means that the injured person can sue any or all the parties involved in making the product.

The Act covers parts and raw materials, and again the manufacturers of both can be liable. In deciding if a product was defective the court will take into account the manner in which the product was marketed, together with any instructions supplied, and the length of production. The essence of the Act is that products should be as safe as it is reasonable to expect. It prevents unfair competition from companies who manage to give low prices only by reducing the safety standards of the product.

11.8   Unsolicited Goods and Services Act 1971

The number of offences of this type has dropped considerably since this Act was passed. Prior to 1971 many companies relied upon this type of inertia selling, sending goods that had not been ordered, in the hope that consumers or individuals would accept and pay. Unsolicited goods and services need not be paid for, and can be retained by the recipient if not collected within six months. It is an offence for the supplier to make demands for payment provided the goods are unsolicited.

11.9   Food Advertising, Labelling

The food manufacturer, retailer or supplier must be aware of the minefield of regulations surrounding the sale or marketing of any food product. Before offering a food product for sale to the consumer, any marketing department would be well advised to check with the local Trading Standards officer.

It is an offence under the Food and Drugs Act 1955 to apply a false description to any food, or to mislead the buyer about its nature, composition, quality or substance. This includes any dietary or nutritional values – so care must be taken with comments such as '10% added bran' or 'no artificial additives'. In conjunction with the Weights and Measures Act general instructions are laid down for:

- brand names or trade marks;
- naming of food products;
- illustrations and graphics;
- flash offer panels;
- listing of ingredients;
- maker's name and address.

In addition to the areas above, there are many special regulations relating to specific groups of food.

11.10 Contract Law

A company or organisation is in business to sell goods or services to others. In so doing, contracts are made with customers. The displaying of goods in a catalogue, in a window, on posters, or in the form of samples is not creating a contract, but is called an 'invitation to treat'. In other words, the prospective customer can make an offer to the owner which may, or may not, be accepted.

There is no general requirement placed upon a company to sell any item to another individual or company if it does not wish to, unless the refusal is based on sexual or racial discrimination. This is just one of the many complexities surrounding the law of contract.

How many traders stop to consider if the person purchasing an item is 'over 18, sober and of sound mind'? The letter of the law states that any person under 18, a drunken person or a mental patient can legally only be made to pay for what are defined as necessaries – usually seen as food and clothing. In practice traders will not always ask the age of a customer, unless the law forbids the sale of certain products to young persons. However, the legal age does affect the granting of credit facilities.

Making an offer

An offer can be made in writing, by word of mouth, or by some other form indicating the offer is accepted. Any terms or conditions must be made clear at the time, or before the contract is made.

Contract breach

A breach of contract by a seller may occur if:

- goods are defective;
- services are badly performed or incomplete;
- the goods supplied are different to those offered as samples, are not of merchantable quality, or unfit for their intended purpose;
- goods are delivered past the time agreed.

A breach of contract by the buyer may occur if:

- goods are not paid for;
- goods are refused or returned because of a change of mind on the part of the buyer.

Sale of Goods Act 1979

This Act seeks to control and quantify the tens of thousands of sales of goods undertaken every day, and to bring a degree of control to the complex areas of contract law. These can be regulated by legal contracts and conditions, which is commonly the case in industrial purchases, or they can be contracts as simple as stepping on to a public transport vehicle expecting to be transported to your destination. The Act determines a number of different areas relating to all contracts, covering transfer of title, ownership, definition of contract, fitness for purpose, etc. In marketing, the most likely area to merit attention is the fitness for purpose section 14(2), where the goods supplied must be of 'merchantable quality'.

Supply of Goods and Services Act 1982

This Act covers goods provided as part of a service, e.g. paint by a decorator.

Merchantable quality

Goods of any kind are of merchantable quality if they are fit for the purpose for which goods of that type are commonly brought, having regard to any description applied to them, the price, and all other relevant circumstances.

The court will take into account the price of the product and the description and compare it with similar types of goods which are available. It is obviously not fair to compare a high-priced product with a similar but lower-priced item. We expect to pay a higher price for quality, but at the same time we expect a better service, over a longer time. The court will take this into account when deciding if the product is of merchantable quality. There is no implied condition of merchantable quality if:

- any defects are specifically drawn to the buyer's attention before the contract is made
  or
- the buyer examines the goods for any defects, which could be revealed if examined, before the contract is made.

Fitness for purpose

If the buyer makes known to the seller any particular purpose for which the goods are required, then they must be reasonably fit for the purpose. If the purpose for which they are purchased is not explained to the seller, or if the buyer does not rely on the seller's skill and judgement, then the fitness for purpose qualification cannot apply. The marketing department should ensure that if a product is specified to a certain standard, or for a certain purpose, then the product should then be capable of meeting or exceeding that standard of performance. Service organisations carry a grave responsibility for their service to meet the required standard.

Sales by sample

The buyers will expect any goods supplied to them to be identical in all respects to any samples offered prior to the order. Marketing will need to ensure that the sales representatives do not carry samples which have been given additional treatment – special polishing, extra coatings, etc. Any sample must accurately reflect the quality of the whole.

Corresponding to description

If the buyer has purchased goods or services without the opportunity to inspect, then when supplied they must accurately match the description given. This can also apply when goods are inspected, but the inspection would not show an obvious false description.

Example

If a metal casting was described in the company literature or advertising as meeting a minimum standard of strength, but upon testing in a laboratory situation proved to be below strength, then the goods can be rejected in total.

Examination of goods

A customer must be given a reasonable opportunity to examine the goods to confirm that they correspond to the items detailed or expected under the contract. Once accepted they cannot be rejected unless a serious defect appears which was not apparent at the time of acceptance.

Obligations to replace goods

A buyer does not have a legal right to have the goods replaced. If the products prove defective, then the full or part amount can be refunded in cash. The seller is not expected to take back goods if it is merely due to a change of mind. In the marketing of special products or offers, the situation may arise where all the products have been sold, and none remain. In this case the advantage to the seller of the cash refund can be clearly understood.

Other contract terms

The court will possibly uphold certain contract terms if they can be shown to be reasonable. These could include terms which seek to limit the liability for loss or damage arising from negligence, or terms where a supplier seeks to limit the liability for descriptions, quality or fitness of items sold.

This liability may be investigated by any following court procedure to see if the liability limitation is within the resources and insurance levels of the supplier. A trader cannot limit liability for death or injury to the consumer arising from the trader's negligence.

Advertising

There is a current British Code of Advertising Practice, which does not yet carry the authority of the law, but it would be well for the marketeer to ensure that he or she conforms to the standards expected.

The Code recommends:

(1) all advertisements should be legal, decent, honest and truthful;
(2) all advertisements should be prepared with a sense of responsibility to the consumer;
(3) all advertisements should conform to the principles of fair competition as generally accepted in business.

Chapter 12

Franchising

One of the growth areas of marketing is the development of franchising in the distribution and service industries. An increasing number of British and foreign companies are adopting this method.

12.1 Terminology

To understand franchising we must firstly understand the terms used:

Franchise – the specific business idea, service or product.
Franchisor – the individual or company offering a franchise.
Franchisee – the individual or company taking a franchise.

Example

Colonel Saunders' Kentucky Fried Chicken is a fast food which relies on a particular method of precooking to give the required tenderness plus the application of a special coating to the chicken, and subsequent deep frying. Heavily advertised and marketed, the product/service combination proved popular with the consumer. Colonel Saunders offered the business idea on a franchise basis. The franchisee is offered the exclusive opportunity to operate a franchise in a designated geographical area, supported by the national marketing effort of the Saunders management.

What is franchising?

Put simply, franchising is the licensing of a business idea to another individual or company (franchisee), enabling them to benefit from the marketing strength of the originating company (franchisor), yet still retain the day-to-day control of the business and a large percentage of the profits resulting from the operation of the franchise.

12.2 Advantages of the Franchising System for the Franchisee

1. *Operates under a nationally known name and trade mark.* In theory, the franchisee has the immediate advantage of trading under the banner of a ready-made business idea, which is already operating under a nationally recognised brand or trading name. In practice the prospective franchisee must ensure that this is in fact the case, by carefully checking the existence and trading figures of the existing franchises in operation.

2. *Customers can immediately recognise the company and be confident in the reputation enjoyed.* Franchises take particular care to ensure that all products or services offered to the consumer or to a business meet predetermined set standards. This ensures that clients are able to relate the level of quality experienced to all similar franchises.

3. *Local franchisee benefits from the national publicity and promotion.* The strength of the franchise lies in the capacity for undertaking publicity and public relations on behalf of all the franchises spread throughout the country. Where an individual company may find this task beyond its capabilities, this task is more easily undertaken by the head office of the franchise. Promotions can more easily be undertaken as the buying power of the franchise is greater than that of any individual company.

4. *Nationally recognised product or service.* Buyers expect products to be of a certain standard, and to be consistently so. In this respect, customers have more confidence in nationally recognised products and services. The franchisee, under the same trade name, shares in this collective consumer confidence and loyalty.

5. *Standard product and quality, with no variation.* Standards are maintained throughout the chain of franchises by ensuring

that products are only supplied from reliable and tested suppliers. Part of the binding franchise agreement made between the two parties will specify particular suppliers, more often the franchisor exclusively. The success of the McDonald fast-food outlets is based on the speed of service, cleanliness, value and product quality being identical throughout the country.

6. *Bulk purchase advantage and improved purchasing practice.* The specification of a quality standard enables a large franchise operation to enter into worthwhile negotiations with suppliers of raw or manufactured materials. Bulk purchasing enables preferential prices to be negotiated – the benefits of which can be passed on to the franchisee.

7. *Proven system of operating the franchise gained from past experience.* The greatest advantage to the franchisee is the operation of a marketing/production/service system which has a proven record of success. Provided the operator conforms to the standards of operation set through the franchisor's training courses and manuals, then profitability is assured.

8. *Installation of a proven management system and control.* Certain franchises will negotiate a licence or royalty payment based on turnover, and in order to check and control this amount they will install an effective management control system covering all areas of the business. Inexperienced business-persons may well find this assistance of considerable value.

9. *Assistance in financing the business, due to the proven viability of the business idea.* While the initial investment required for a franchise can be considerable, finance is often more easily obtained due to the proven record of other franchises. Banks and other financial institutions are likely to be convinced of the viability based on figures obtained from other franchises.

10. *Assistance in deciding site location and selection of suitable business property.* Franchisees who are seeking suitable properties to carry out their operations will have established requirements to ensure the success of the franchise. Their advice and assistance in purchasing or leasing properties from which to operate will be based on the turnover records and success of other similar business ventures.

11. *Individual design of fixtures and fittings to co-ordinate with national image of franchise.* Company colours, style of fittings, design of signs, and the general appearance of the franchise will be co-ordinated with the national standard to ensure that the successful image is repeated through all operations.

Franchisees will be helped by the provision of authorised shopfitters, equipment suppliers, van-leasing companies, signwriters and subsidiary service companies offering such things as security systems and stationery.

12. *Advice on the promotion of the business, assistance with marketing, advertising and sales promotion.* Promotion of the business – especially during the initial opening period – will be offered by the franchisor. This should continue throughout the period of the franchise, by means of joint promotion/ advertising schemes.

13. *Advice on selection of stock, stock-holding figures and market research.* Through the management control system operated by the franchisor, figures will be available to the new franchisee showing the relative sales of each of the products or services on offer. These figures will be based on the results of market research undertaken in successful franchises. Through these figures franchisees can purchase products or offer services which are proven successes in the market.

Example

Dyno-rod drain-clearing franchises could require a minimum size of business property, sufficient to store up to three vehicles and associated equipment, situated in a town or district with predominantly pre-war housing and with large industrial estates within a ten mile radius of the property.

12.3 Advantages of the Franchising System to the Franchisor

Just as the franchise system offers advantages to the franchisee in providing a ready-made business, so the system offers distinct benefits to the organisation offering the franchised business idea.

1. *Produces additional investment capital.* The sale of the franchise package releases additional capital which can be utilised to increase production, improve marketing expenditure or expand operations.

2. *Devolves management to a local level.* With a large number of similar businesses the difficulty lies in ensuring that management is carried out at an effective level. Franchising

brings the level of management as close as is possible to the actual consumer or buyer. This produces a more effective management style, aware of costs and local sales developments.

3. *Individual ownership brings motivation.* The franchisor's business develops faster through the motivation of individual owners. This motivation is greater than would be the case by installing a manager/ess.

4. *Reduced operating costs.* The use of a franchise reduces the overall running costs of operating a large number of outlets. The franchisor can then concentrate on the expansion of the business rather than the installation of increasingly top-heavy control systems.

5. *Acceptance in the community as a local business.* Customers seeing a known local business person operating his or her own individual franchise will respond better than to an unknown manager/ess. Expansion of the franchise is more likely to succeed in the hands of a local person who is aware of the particular quirks and foibles of his fellow-citizens.

6. *Limited payroll and insurance costs.* The major problem in any expansion plan is the responsibility of employing extra staff, with the resulting increased payroll and insurance costs. By franchising, these costs become the responsibility of the individual proprietor and are not part of the costs of the originating company.

7. *Better communications.* Communications are always improved by the use of shorter lines which exist in the simple franchisee-franchisor arrangement.

8. *Fast and selective distribution.* The product or service will be offered through a limited number of effective distributorships, each within a specified area of the country. This aids the effective marketing of the franchise and prevents clashes between competing distributors.

12.4   Background to Franchising

Franchising itself is no sure guarantee of instant business growth for either party to the agreement. In common with all new business ventures the odds are always heavily against success. Figure 12.1 shows graphically how the difficulties increase through the years:

Fig.12.1 *Failed Business Ventures*

Years in business	Number of failed business ventures
1	1 in 12.6
2	1 in 9.7
3	1 in 10.0
4	1 in 9.9
5	1 in 9.61
10	1 in 8.4

12.5 Legal and Business Aspects of Franchising

The franchise binds both parties to an agreement over the exact liabilities each undertakes. Normally the aggreement will be based on an initial investment of capital in the form of a franchise fee representing a payment for:

1 supply of any specialised equipment;
2 initial stock of products;
3 documentation;
4 advice and expertise;
5 use of trade and brand names;
6 the right to utilise the designs, layouts, patents, working arrangements, equipment, processes and products developed by the franchisor;
7 the right to use the central services of the franchisor;
8 the right to operate in a certain location or area without competition from the franchisor or any other franchisee.

In addition to the payment of the agreed fee, which is usually based upon the area or size of operation, the franchisee also agrees to:

1 advance the sales of the franchisor's products/services;
2 maintain the standard quality of products/services;
3 co-operate and co-ordinate business activities with those of the franchisor and other franchisees;
4 uphold the reputation of the franchisor and care for the image of the outlet.
5 make certain agreed payments to the franchisor.

Any contract resulting from an agreement should clearly define the conditions related to the transfer, termination or renewal of the franchise operation.

Franchising is a developing method of marketing, but must only be undertaken as the result of taking professional advice from a solicitor or accountant. Not all franchises offer the required marketing or expertise to ensure success, and in fact are merely a cover for an investment in stock, usually sold at a higher than normal price. Should the franchise have none of the attributes mentioned in Section 12.2, then care should be taken over the investment.

Further information and advice on the advantages of franchising can be obtained from the British Franchise Association.

Assignment

You are interested in a new franchise being offered on the UK market for a patented process and equipment used for the preservation of wood. Suitable for all types of household and garden construction, it produces a waterproof, rot-proof, invisible coating which will protect any wooden item for a minimum period of 15 years. The minimum investment required is approximately £25 000, which includes the provision of a suitable vehicle, spray equipment and preserving materials, together with initial training, and assistance with promotion and advertising.

You are scheduled to meet the UK sales manager of the franchisor at 10.30 am in a week's time for an initial fact-finding meeting. You intend to send her a list of the particular questions you would need answering before deciding if the franchise represents a worthwhile investment of your capital. Prepare a list of suitable questions which you consider would need to be answered by the franchisor concerning the strengths and weaknesses of the franchise system.

PART III

SALES AND SELLING METHODS

Chapter 13

The Sales Function

The sales force and associated sales staff act as the final stage in communicating the marketing strategy to the customer. However effectively the tools of marketing are utilised, at some stage of the communications process with the customer the personal face to face interplay is required. An awareness of the skills of personal selling is necessary for all those involved in marketing, and in this chapter we shall study the role and operation of the sales force.

13.1   Organisation

Every medium-sized organisation or company will have within the management team staff who are responsible for the control of the company sales force. Larger UK and multinational corporations will ensure involvement of the sales function in management decision-making by the appointment of a sales director as part of the board. Smaller organisations may combine the sales function with that of marketing.

Control of the sales force in both cases will normally be through national sales managers, operating through several regional managers. Regional managers control a number of field sales managers, who in turn ensure the effective utilisation of the field sales force on a day-today basis. Figure 13.1 shows a typical sales organisation chart for three different types of company.

Esso Petroleum UK is the second largest oil company in the United kingdom, marketing a range of lubricants and fuels to account customers. Their sales efforts are directed to ensuring customers are made aware of the full range of company products, encouraged to order, and informed of new developments. The company employ sales representatives, divided into separate markets controlled by field sales managers. The field

Fig.13.1 *Sales Organisation Chart*

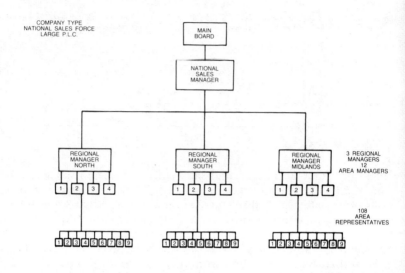

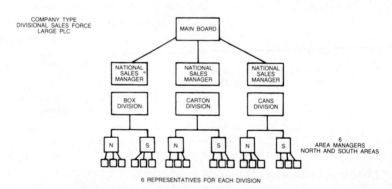

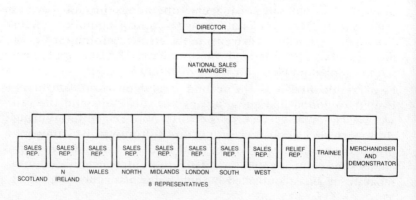

sales managers report to national sales managers. The product range is extensive, with considerable technical knowledge being required. Representatives operate in each specific market segment: retail, industrial, aviation and fuels.

Makro UK is the largest cash and carry wholesaler, dealing with a wide range of retail outlets, offering groceries, confectionery and consumer durables. The company sales force is responsible for introducing new accounts to the services available. Each sales representative is attached to a specific outlet and covers customers within the market area. Representatives normally undertake approx. 600 visits per month to new and existing clients.

Everest Double Glazing operates in the competitive domestic market, installing double-glazed window units in over 20 000 homes and offices each year. The sales force of 200 undertake calls each week, usually by prior appointment, the leads being gained by customer response to advertising campaigns. A company sales force will be organised to achieve a specific purpose, dependent upon the company marketing objectives. Each company will set individual marketing targets, some seeking maximum distribution of the product range to existing customers, others seeking new customers, while many will seek to combine these two functions.

13.2 Types of Sales Force

In understanding the sales force we must first consider the differing types of employment found within the profession, and the personal characteristics needed by sales staff to achieve the marketing plan. A major point for consideration before employing full-time sales representatives is the high cost involved. Figure 13.2 shows the annual cost of operating a single sales representative.

The figures shown do not include the initial costs of providing a company vehicle, samples and sales aids for demonstrating to customers, and the costs of induction and company training. It will be clear that in order to generate a profit for the company, a high sales turnover is required merely to cover these annual expenses. This factor is instrumental in persuading many companies to seek other forms of sales representation.

Fig. 13.2 *The Cost of Employing a Salesperson*

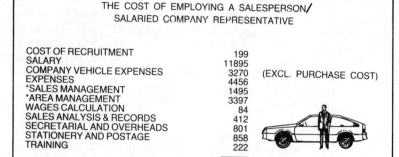

THE COST OF EMPLOYING A SALESPERSON/
SALARIED COMPANY REPRESENTATIVE

COST OF RECRUITMENT	199	
SALARY	11895	
COMPANY VEHICLE EXPENSES	3270	(EXCL. PURCHASE COST)
EXPENSES	4456	
*SALES MANAGEMENT	1495	
*AREA MANAGEMENT	3397	
WAGES CALCULATION	84	
SALES ANALYSIS & RECORDS	412	
SECRETARIAL AND OVERHEADS	801	
STATIONERY AND POSTAGE	858	
TRAINING	222	
TOTAL COST	27089	

OR £589 EACH WEEK

APPROXIMATE FIGURES FOR REPRESENTATIVES IN THE GROCERY,
HARDWARE, CONFECTIONERY AND PHARMACEUTICAL INDUSTRIES
*LARGER COMPANIES

13.3   Company Sales Representatives

The economy of the United Kingdom presently provides employment for over 30 000 full-time company sales representatives. A typical sales force can vary in size from a single person to 150 staff, dependent upon sales turnover and organisational requirements. A company sales representative's duties will be primarily as sales negotiators but, in addition, they will also be required to act as company diplomats, ensuring that client satisfaction and company service levels are maintained. The high cost of representation may be partly offset by utilising the sales force in a variety of other roles, such as manning exhibitions, addressing consumer or client groups, or collecting outstanding credit accounts.

Salaries and benefits

Company sales representatives are a highly-paid professional body, responsible through their selling efforts for the employment of 35 production workers. As such, they benefit from salaries between £7000 to £15 000. In addition, normal business expenses incurred in the performance of their duties are reimbursed by the company. A company vehicle is provided, purchased or leased, with all fuel, oil and servicing costs being met.

In order to encourage the maximum involvement and effort by sales staff, company management will offer a wide range of staff incentives. These will vary from a simple commission structure to specially designed competitions or bonus schemes.

13.4   Sales Agents and Associates

Sales agents and sales associates are utilised by organisations with smaller production or turnover, or those not wishing to employ a large number of full-time representatives.

Sales agents

Sales agents are not considered as employees of the company, and are therefore not covered by employment legislation, and for all intents and purposes are seen as self-employed. Sales agents operate on sales commission, which varies according to the value of the product. For products which have a ready sale in the market, for example, grocery products or electrical consumer goods, the normal commission will be around 7.5% to 10% of invoice value. On items with a higher capital value, such as computers or capital equipment, the commission can rise to 15% of the installed value. An agent's revenue from commission must be substantial enough to cover on-the-road expenses plus salary. To ensure that it is, they will often act on behalf of a number of companies operating in the same market segment.

Sales associates

Certain companies, especially those dealing with the general public on a door-to-door basis – double glazing, home improvement, life assurance – have developed the role of the sales associate. In these cases the representative remains self-employed, receiving commission on sales made. The company will, however, provide qualified leads (names of prospective clients obtained through other marketing efforts), office and telephone facilities, sales training and secretarial support.

In general most companies operate in an ethical manner, but

prospective sales representatives should be aware of certain companies who offer unusually high rates of commission or the prospect of high earnings. All too often the payment can depend on numerous conditions which are unlikely to be met easily by the agent, with either a high initial investment in product samples, or considerable payment being required for an exclusive sales territory.

Certain companies will seek to recruit new sales agents by offering high annual commission earnings. It would be wise for any potential sales agent to consider why a company would seek to offer total commission greater than the cost of employing a full-time salaried representative (see Figure 13.2). While the position of sales agent or associate offers an entrée into selling, those persons with little previous sales experience, or anyone currently unemployed, should check carefully into the background of the prospective employer.

Example

Mr Trevor Dolman acts as sales agent for a number of companies supplying products to the fishing tackle and sporting gun trade. His list of client companies is selected to ensure that a clash of interests cannot occur. He offers his customers British fishing tackle and clothing, Spanish shotguns, German fishing reels, French fishing lines, and a wide variety of products from smaller producers. Individually, none of his client companies could afford to employ him as a full-time company sales representative, nor could Trevor afford to act exclusively for one. However, by representing a number of agencies, Trevor is able to offer his customers a wider range of products. He acts as a contact source between customers and the suppliers for whom he acts, dealing with any queries or problems that arise. In addition he provides professional representation for those companies who would otherwise be unable to afford the services of an individual representative. All three participants benefit from this arrangement. Trevor enjoys the freedom of arranging his working day to suit his requirements. His customers benefit from the personal contact with their suppliers, and the manufacturers are assured of first-class representation from a self-employed representative.

13.5 Van Sales Representatives

Within certain market segments, especially those selling to retail outlets, the use of van sales representatives is common. Partly due to historical reasons, but increasingly to gain the impulse purchase, this area continues to expand in the UK. Representatives are supplied with a suitable commercial vehicle, sufficient in size to carry a representative stock-holding of the company products. The task of a van sales representative is to encourage the buyer to inspect the products and make a purchase, for delivery directly from the vehicle or for supply on the next scheduled visit.

Payment for goods supplied is usually on a cash on delivery basis. This method of selling enables particular market segments to be covered effectively at reasonable cost. In pursuit of larger orders and delivery drops, many companies have neglected the smaller buyer, enabling specialist local suppliers to fill the market gap created by this policy.

13.6 Sales Merchandisers

Usually operating in the retail environment, sales merchandisers act as support staff to the selling efforts of the company representative. Having sold the initial order to the retailer, there is a requirement to ensure that the product is moved rapidly into the hands of the consumer. Normally sales merchandisers are employed on a part-time basis. Their duties are to ensure the shelving and stock fittings displaying the product are fully stocked and correctly organised. In the fast-moving consumer market, increased sales are obtained if the fittings are correctly merchandised. Sales merchandisers also undertake the construction of special promotion displays within stores, in addition to completing stock records and sales statistics.

13.7 Canvassers

A recent development in selling is the increased use of sales canvassers, whose duties are to 'pave the way' for representatives. Canvassers are employed in teams and will mainly restrict their operation to the home-owner. Trained by their employers to make the initial contact with householders, they seek solely to make an appointment for a representative to call and discuss the products at a later date.

Unethical companies will attempt to give the impression that they are undertaking a market research survey in order to gain information concerning the customer's background. Genuine market researchers will carry identification issued by the Market Research Society or similar associations. The normal form of remuneration for sales canvassers is in the form of an appointment bonus payment, sales commission or bonus on the eventual sales value obtained.

13.8   Telephone Sales

In order to improve the effectiveness of the sales effort and to increase the selling-time available to representatives, companies will utilise the technique of telephone selling.

Telephone selling is often misunderstood, in that it is obviously impossible for any company to obtain orders if no initial face to face selling has taken place. No customer would order over the telephone, or forward payment to a supplier, without having taken the opportunity to examine the product or service.

Telephone selling is used to great effect by companies operating in the FMCG market sectors (Fast Moving Consumer Goods) to contact existing customers for orders which might otherwise be lost between the visits of the representative. Once this initial contact has been made by the representative, and an account opened with the supplier, telephone sales staff will contact the buyer at agreed times between visits to ensure the company's product range is kept fully stocked, and is delivered (usually by the next day).

Telephone selling is also used for the making of an initial appointment with prospective clients (known as cold calls). This method allows more effective use of the representative's time, ensuring that visits are made to prospective clients by appointment.

13.9   Party Plan Selling

Introduced into the UK in the mid-sixties from the United States, party-plan selling involves appointed area agents of the company organising selling events or parties. These are held in the home of a selected host who, in return for their efforts in inviting friends, providing light refreshments, ensuring orders are delivered, and collecting payments, is invited to select a gift from the company's range of goods. These gifts rise in value dependent upon the total value of orders taken during the party.

13.10 Mail Order Agents

The mail order market in the UK represents an annual sales turnover in excess of £2½ million each year. The wide range of goods and services are sold by a vast number of individual part-time agents, operating from their homes and usually selling to family and neighbours and friends. Commission only is paid, and rates vary from 10% if taken as a cash payment, to 12% if taken in goods from the company's catalogue. It is unusual for agents to receive any formal sales training, relying instead for their sales on the attraction of the fully-illustrated mail order catalogue and the policy of returning items if unsuitable.

13.11 Retail Sales

Retail has an advantage over other forms of selling, in that the customers have chosen of their own volition to enter the retail outlet. This continuous flow of customers through the shop doors has tended to encourage many sales assistants to under-value the high level of selling skill required in retailing. They incorrectly assume that the benefits of low prices, display techniques and special promotions remove the need to utilise selling methods in persuading the customer to buy.

Despite the efforts of many companies in the retail market, sales assistants with the required professional selling skills tend to be few and far between, resulting in poor turnover, low customer satisfaction, and low self-respect for the role of sales assistant. Even with the highly mechanised retail self-service format, sales assistants are responsible for a wide range of personal selling and communication skills, dealing with customer enquiries, customers returning unsuitable goods, and with the general day-to-day customer relationship.

13.12 What Makes a Successful Salesperson?

Selling and the sales function remains a highly skilled profession, requiring certain qualities and characteristics in those who seek to practise the art. All too often the assumption is falsely made that the only qualities required are 'the gift of the gab', a fund of risqué stories and an extrovert personality. Nothing could be further from the truth, and a recent survey undertaken to discover the qualities inherent in the top 10% of successful sales staff highlighted the following attributes.

Self-motivation

The ability in a salesperson to motivate, or propel themselves mentally towards greater sales efforts is important. Self-motivation requires the utmost self-control to force oneself to carry on with the selling task despite temporary setbacks or failures.

Self-discipline

Research also shows that a salesperson working for an average of eight hours each day will spend as little as 1½ hours engaged in the actual task of selling. In the marketing context, other tasks requiring the salesperson's attention may take priority, thus reducing the amount of time available. These can include:

    collection of outstanding and current credit balances;
    delivery, invoice and account queries from customers;
    completion of company statistical information;
    market intelligence activities and competitor analysis.

The additional time pressures on field sales representatives involved in travelling, waiting to speak with buyers, and general non-selling tasks can result in failure to allocate sufficient time for the face to face contact with clients. If we bear in mind the high cost of a full-time representative, it is apparent that the total profitability of the sales operation can depend on the generation of a considerable sales turnover in a relatively short selling-time. The task therefore requires a high level of self-discipline, involving extended hours, preplanning, preparation, professionalism, and marketing support from the company departments.

Professional training

Training of sales staff is an essential part of the company's marketing effort, although this training is often in the technicalities of the product rather than the skills of selling. High quality training for the sales representative should consist of an initial introduction to the company methods of selling, together with continuous refresher training during his or her sales career.

Technical expertise

Considerable discussion takes place in marketing over the relative merits of employing a person with technical qualifications or expertise, and then instilling the skills of selling through training. Other organisations will seek staff with sales skills, possibly gained in a fast-moving market, and instil the technical knowledge needed. It is wise to bear in mind that all selling takes place at a personal level, with the salesperson appealing to the basic needs inherent in everyone. Provided the required technical knowledge can be translated into benefits for the customer, then technical knowledge can take second place to selling professionalism.

Preplanning

Effective representatives pay particular attention to the need to preplan all selling objectives. Initial research will provide analysis of prospective customers' needs and the most effective way of meeting them from the company product range. Accurate information, gained from prior research and past experience, will ensure maximum effectiveness during the sales sequence. Reflection on past performance on an individual basis will highlight problem areas and ensure that weak areas in the presentation can be improved.

Personality

'The customer is always right' has been quoted for generations as a background comment on selling, implying that the customer always has the final word in any presentation. Far more effective is to consider that the customer may indeed be right, but has not yet been made aware of the facts they require to alter their opinion. In situations where the customer may be heading along the wrong track, the need is for a salesperson with a strong personality to redirect the client.

Sales, by the very nature of the profession, requires a degree of personality to achieve results. Selling is no opportunity for those with little personality, as ineffectiveness communicates itself readily to the customer. At the same time, an overpowering personality will have little chance of success, ruffling more feathers than it smooths. Sales staff should retain their own personality, for good or ill, but pay attention to the following areas:

Confidence – in yourself, your product, and your company

Without this essential attribute, no sales presentation will succeed. If a salesperson lacks confidence in their own ability, the suitability of their products, or the ethics of their company, then they should seek a position where these criteria are met.

Professionalism gained through knowledge of customers

Experience of dealing with all types of customers breeds confidence in the representative. The constant fear of rejection results in a hesitant approach, which is steadily overcome as the representative realises that customers fall into patterns of behaviour.

Strength to overcome setbacks and failure

The ability to return with confidence to the task, despite a day filled with poor results, is essential.

Adaptability

The representative must also be prepared to alter the style, approach, presentation or benefits, and continue to meet the needs defined by the customer.

Empathy

This is the ability to place yourself in the shoes of the customer, and by this gain insight into their requirements: to be able to put the question, 'How would I feel if I were the customer instead of the representative?'

When combined, these attributes should produce a well-rounded and attractive personality, to which the customer can relate. However, it would be extremely unlikely that any salesperson would gain instant rapport with every customer. In rare cases such as this, the salesperson has little option but to accept the situation and seek to transfer the particular customer to a colleague.

Chapter 14

The Basic Sales Skills

Having considered the differing types of sales activity, and the qualities required to carry out the function, we move on to the duties, responsibilities and activities of the salesperson. In general they fall under the following headings, but with variations depending on the particular sphere of selling.

Direct selling activities:
discovering prospective clients and customers;
determining customer needs;
deciding strategy for sales presentation;
presenting company products and services;
offering benefits;
overcoming objections;
closing sales.

Product knowledge:
determining new uses for existing products;
discovering new clients for existing products;
informing marketing of suggested new products;
informing marketing of changes needed to products;
familiarity with company product range;
keeping abreast of product changes and price alterations.

Customer service and relations:
assisting customers with their problems;
arranging additional services for customers;
settling customer complaints;
assisting customers to maintain adequate stock levels;
establishing effective personal relationships with client;
training customers' sales staff, if required;
arranging product information and usage sessions;
maintaining special displays and promotions.

Administration:
keeping records of customer information and calls made;
carrying out routine correspondence;
following up enquiries;
obtaining display and merchandising materials;
checking customer credit ratings;
controlling travel, telephone and other expenses;
communicating items of interest to market intelligence;
organising the sales area;
arranging call frequencies and patterns.

We need to examine each activity in greater detail in order to fully appreciate the daily routine of a typical salesperson.

14.1   Direct Selling Activities

Discovering prospective clients and customers

Prospecting for customers is essential for the continued progression of the company sales effort. Most companies will have an existing client base, possibly built up over many years. Each year this base of customers can be expected to decline through customers ceasing to trade, or moving away from the sales area. The sales representatives from competitor companies will also be attacking the client base, attempting to win orders by encouraging buyers to change suppliers. The average percentage reduction in customers is around 18% each year, highlighting the need for constant prospecting by the representative.

To compete with this reduction, the salesperson will be constantly seeking new customers who have moved into the area or who have not been previously contacted. Names of prospective customers can be obtained from a variety of sources, including:

- local chambers of trade and commerce;
- replies to advertising or direct mail campaigns;
- planning applications made to local councils;
- information from satisfied customers (third party referrals);
- advertisements in papers seeking employees for new businesses;
- Register of Electors from councils or local library;

- purchase of computerised listings of new companies;
- business directories (*Kompass*, *Kelly*, etc.);
- visual observation of new developments and new companies.

Once new clients are discovered, the representative is expected to make the initial contact and to book an appointment with the customer to introduce the company range of products. Many representatives consider the task of 'cold calling' is the most demanding of all sales activities, requiring high levels of confidence, sales professionalism and product knowledge. Given the inherent difficulties, successfully converting 'cold calls' is a source of considerable satisfaction and a boost to the representative's morale.

Determining customer needs

Before determining customers' needs, a certain amount of information about the company should be gained before the interview by the use of directories and similar sources, namely:

- type of business product service;
- name of contact to be approached;
- current company priorities;
- current supplier being used.

Selling skills are based upon question techniques. We are all blessed with two ears and one mouth, and therefore we should listen for twice as long as we speak. All too often inexperienced representatives consider they are required to present a section from a Shakespeare play, allowing no interruption or contribution from their audience. We sell by asking direct and indirect questions of our customer, for questions are the fastest way to get to the facts.

Direct questions can be answered by either yes or no, and are used to check on customer reaction to the proposals.

Indirect questions cannot be answered by a simple yes or no. They give the representative more information, and encourage the customer to talk.

Example

Direct question: Do you enjoy sports?
Indirect question: Which sport do you enjoy most?

Indirect questions will usually begin with who, what, why, when, where, how, or will require the customer to decide on an alternative (double choice).

1 Who is the person in charge of your production?
2 What range of products do you carry at present?
3 Why do you feel our product will fit your needs?
4 When would you like our quotation?
5 Where will the machine be installed?
6 How would you wish to pay for the stereo?

Questions 4, 5 and 6 could be asked with an alternative, giving the customer a double choice, as follows:
   Add to 4: Would Friday be OK, or would Wednesday be better?
   Add to 5: Is it better in reception, or in your office?
   Add to 6: We can offer hire purchase, or extended credit.

The customer is offered alternative choices, but it can be seen that by utilising two options the hesitant buyer is encouraged to make a positive decision. Never offer less than two choices to any customer. By asking structured questions, we discover the customer's needs. Once these needs are ascertained, by using the skills of selling, we structure the presentation to provide the answers.

Deciding strategy for sales presentation

Having discovered customer needs by question techniques and prior research, we need to decide upon the direction of our presentation. In order to sell, the sales representative must appeal to a customer's self-interest. The presentation is therefore structured to take account of the selling power inherent in:

basic needs –	the basic essentials required by all customers;
safety –	freedom from pain or discomfort;
love and belonging –	acceptance and emotional relationships;
esteem –	prestige, recognition, status or fame;
self-actualisation –	being someone or something.

By noting the responses given to the initial questions, we can determine the most likely appeal to the customer's self-interest, and adapt the presentation to suit the individual needs.

Example

Philip Bond, the fleet sales representative of the local Ford main dealer, asks his customers carefully structured 'search questions' in order to discover their buying needs. He will begin by seeking to discover the customer's present vehicle, and the qualities with which they are satisfied. Other vital areas to discover are those with which the customer is dissatisfied.

He found that the customer is well pleased with the comfort and fittings in their present vehicle, but less pleased with the reliability and performance. Philip decided that the most effective method of meeting the customer's self- needs was to emphasise the ease of servicing, freedom from breakdowns and pre-testing of the Ford range.

His presentation pointed out to the customer all the features of the vehicle which appealed to the self-need for safety, and the freedom from the pain and discomfort of a vehicle breakdown. By stressing these features, together with the equivalent comfort and fittings, he is able to convert the customer to his range of vehicles.

Presenting company products and services

As an aid to presenting the company products and services, the marketing department of a company will assist by providing a wide range of promotional support. This could be in the form of specially produced high quality brochures, catalogues, price lists, demonstration samples, or even portable video recorders for illustrating technical products or processes.

Offering benefits

Every product or service offered by a company has a number of individual features exclusive to that item. In presenting our product or service, we turn those chosen features into benefits to the customer by examining the manner in which the feature performs its job. To do this, we take the feature we wish to present and consider the function of the feature (what does it do?). Having decided what the feature does, we turn the function into a benefit (what does it do for the customer?).

Example		
De luxe washing machine		
Feature	*Function* (What does it do?)	*Benefit* (for customer)
Stainless steel drum	Prevents corrosion Stops rust Lasts longer	Prevents your clothes being stained Saves you money
Half-wash cycle	Uses less hot water Washes quicker Uses less powder	Costs you less to run Saves you time Saves you money

Let us see how one of these examples forms part of a typical sales presentation:

The de luxe model of this washing machine has a special half-wash cycle, controlled by a microchip processor, which means that this machine will save you time and money.

If we analyse the sequence of this short sales benefit, we can expect the customer to think:

. . . half-wash cycle . . . so what!
. . . microchip processor . . . that's interesting.
. . . will save you time and money . . . now that's what I want!

The inexperienced salesperson may seek to impress the customer with technical knowledge, or assume, that the customer understands their technical jargon. This has the effect of making customers feel inferior, and prevents two-way communication. The salesperson must convert every technical point into a benefit for the customer. Only in this way can the sales presentation prove effective, allowing customers to meet their needs by purchasing your product or service.

Assignment

Pick a product with which you are familiar, possibly one that you have recently purchased. Discover three features the product possesses. Convert those features into benefits for the customer. Ensure each benefit contains the word 'you'.

Overcoming objections

It would be surprising if a customer accepted every single statement made by a salesperson without comment. Objections can arise at any time during the sales conversation, when the customer's opinion differs from the salesperson's. They should be welcomed as a sign that the customer is interested but has perhaps misunderstood what was said, or requires proof of a claim being made.

Experience will show that objections fall into certain categories, usually based on price or fear of buying. The sales person should therefore build the answers to these expected objections into their sales presentation, and refute them before they arise. Objections should be answered by using additional product knowledge, converted into benefits for the customer. These are then restated to show that the advantages outweigh the apparent drawbacks. We use the technique of apparent agreement or 'yes – but' to show understanding of their point of view. This has the effect of relaxing the objection and giving time for thought before replying. It also shows courtesy in appreciating the customer's point of view.

It is dangerous, when dealing with objections, to give the impression of insincerity by answering too quickly or being glib with your reply, as this causes the customer to suspect the objection is not being answered truthfully. Objections should never be answered by arguing, or denying the problem exists.

The salesperson may win the argument, but will surely lose the customer.

Example

'I quite see your point of view, Mr Porter; what you say is absolutely true. But have you considered the extra years of life this machine offers . . . '

If necessary, you should clarify what the customer says by repeating the objection, to show that the point of view is clearly understood.

'Mr Porter, you feel that the machine is, in fact, too large for your needs? . . . I quite see your point of view, but . . .'

All too often customers will raise objections to disguise the real reason for not buying. They may not care to admit that the price is more than they can afford, and so raise an objection on a technical point in the belief that this will divert attention. Having answered the objection, ask outright, 'You still seem hesitant; what is the other point that bothers you?'

An objection, if not dealt with to the satisfaction of the customer, will not disappear. It will reappear at a later time phrased in a different context. If the objection makes a comparison between your product and that of a competitor, never seek to disparage the competition, as this could well offend the customer's sense of fair play. The most common objection raised concerns the price of an item, and causes special worry to most sales staff. A most effective method is to present the price more favourably by dividing it by the number of years' life, or the cost per day, per mile, or any other relevant figure.

Closing sales

At a certain stage during the presentation the customer will express interest in the product or proposition by making a verbal or visual buying signal. Representatives should attune themselves to these signals and respond in a positive fashion, possible by attempting to close the sale. Typical verbal buying signals could include a customer making statements similar to these examples:

Do you supply this washing machine in a light blue?
How long is the guarantee on this machine?
How fast is delivery?

The initial reaction on the part of the representative may be to answer such a question in a factual manner. If it is realised that the statement is a buying signal, then a different form of answer is the first stage in closing the sale. Try using the following in response to the buying signals above:

Do you want one in light blue?
You can have a free 12-month warranty, or extend it for two further years by paying a small premium. Which do you prefer?
Delivery would be on a Wednesday or Friday. Which would you prefer?

This type of trial close is based upon offering the customer your choice of two possible answers, each of which is a positive response. If a trial close should be answered with a turn-down, then carry on by selling further benefits.

Differing forms of close, equally effective if used with sufficient confidence, are the summary close and the bonus close.

Summary close

The representative proceeds to summarise the major points on which the client has agreed the product offers a benefit, noting the points on paper with the client:

'We agree that this machine offers higher production rates . . . improved quality control . . . less wastage . . . and lower running costs . . . now, is there any reason why you should not order immediately?

Bonus close

Following the sales presentation, the representative retains one further benefit to be used as a final extra 'closer'. This could be an extra discount, extended warranty, or perhaps free delivery. Let us examine the use of this close in a final sequence:

'Mr Marsh, I am happy to say that if you order from me today, I can arrange for your machine to be installed completely free of any charge. Now all I need is details of your delivery address . . . '

Closing the sale is one of the most difficult areas of selling, requiring a high degree of determination on the part of the representative. Success in selling will come only from using professional closing techniques, gained by continuous practice and practical experience.

Warning: It is all too easy to offer a percentage discount off the selling price in order to close the sale. It should be borne clearly in mind that large discounts merely compensate for poor selling methods. The table in Figure 14.1 shows the amount of additional sales turnover required to produce the same amount of profit to a company.

Fig. 14.1   *Discount Table*

When considering giving a discount						
Your Gross Profit Margin	▶10%	15%	20%	25%	30%	40%
Reduce your price by 2%	25%	15%	11%	9%	7%	5%
Reduce your price by 5%	100%	50%	33%	25%	20%	14%
Reduce your price by 10%	–	200%	100%	67%	50%	33%
Reduce your price by 15%	–	–	300%	150%	100%	33%
	▲ Percentage sales must increase ▲					

Example
Your company manufactures a product giving a gross profit of 20%, and you consider giving a discount on each item of 2%.

   If you did decide to give this rather small discount, the chart shows that you would need to increase sales by a further 11%, in order to provide the same amount of gross profit to the company.

14.2   Product Knowledge

Determining new uses for existing products

As part of the general progress of the marketing policy, representatives act as the eyes and ears of the company. During their daily sales calls they have the opportunity to uncover new uses for their products. This could be information gained during conversation with users, many of whom utilise the product in unexpected ways. Larger organisations will often have a specific market intelligence department responsible for analysis of the market, either through desk research or actual research.

Discovering new clients for existing products

New clients for existing products could be the discovery of an untapped market segment whereby a simple product alteration or development could provide worthwhile additional sales.

Many products presently on sale to the consumer originated within the industrial market. Packaging in a different style or smaller quantity may be all that is required. Reports on suggested new client approaches should normally be cleared with sales management before approach. Marketing departments would expect to be involved over allocation of budgets, sales promotion and advertising before entering a new specialist market.

Informing marketing of suggested new products

Sales representatives are stricken with the firm belief that a new product will often improve the competitive market position of a company. Requests usually originate from the field for new products to beat the competition, often based on the 'me too' concept of marketing. Before a product can be marketed, the field sales force must prove a demand exists. Because a competitor has entered the market with a new product, there is no automatic necessity to follow suit.

Representatives should ensure that a note is made of any customer requests for products. If a sufficient number of genuine enquiries are received, the information should be forwarded to marketing for the consideration of the product planning or research and development department. Provided the product meets the company marketing policy and is successful in passing through the checks mentioned in Chapter 4, then the sales force will bear ultimate responsibility for gaining the required sales. In retail sales the use of customer request forms are common, allowing marketing management to keep abreast of customer requirements. Even without the use of these forms, prudent management will encourage reporting of customer requests. Single isolated requests are of little value, but when examined can often show a gap in the existing market.

Informing marketing of changes needed to products

All company products are subject to the need for change, as explained in Chapter 2, as part of the product life-cycle.

Competitors will be marketing products designed to reduce the market share of the representative's company. Special promotions will be used by competitors for a short-term boost to their sales. Discounts will be offered, and the whole range of below-the-line activity will be called into operation to gain market share. Representatives will be aware of these activities, and of the possible effect upon their sales turnover. By keeping their field sales manager informed of developments in the field, the marketing department can undertake appropriate counteraction.

These counteractivities are often merely a cosmetic change to the packaging or to the price structure. Each is designed to keep and gain market or brand share increases. Representatives should be informed of these proposed changes and encouraged to take full advantage of the projected sales increases.

Representatives in the field are meeting and consulting with a constant flow of customers, learning of market trends, competitor activity, and generally getting a feel of the particular market they operate in. Despite this, selling remains a lonely profession, with the representative having little opportunity to discuss progress with colleagues, or, in many larger companies, being allowed to communicate with the marketing department.

The secret lies in effective communication in both directions. The marketing department should attempt to restrict their demands for market information from the representatives, asking only for information which is not available from other sources. Too many requests for information from the sales force has a negative result. Representatives, if under pressure to forward apparently non-essential information, statistics or results of marketing efforts, will tend to forward false or incorrect information.

Marketing can assist and prevent these problems by undertaking field visits, thus ensuring that the representatives, area managers and sales staff are kept fully informed of marketing plans. During these visits much valuable information can be gained. Field sales visits by marketing executives play a major part in boosting the morale of the sales force by creating the correct impression that head office listens to comments from those whose task it is to produce sales turnover each and every day.

Familiarity with company product range

Returning to our example of Esso Petroleum, we find that the company product range extends over 1000 different products. If we take into account the variety of formulations for differing uses, the product range reaches 5000.

No single representative could be expected to remember that amount of product information. To assist the field sales force operating in specialist markets, the Esso Petroleum marketing, production and research departments co-operate to produce a series of information sheets. These sheets give technical information and recommendations, enabling the representative to quickly discover the product most suitable for the customer's needs. Regular product information sheet updates are forwarded direct to the representatives, and it is their duty to familiarise themselves with the new applications. All representatives should ensure their knowledge of the company products is current and relevant and they have the required knowledge to offer recommendations to new or existing clients. Of equal importance is the need to convert the product features into benefits.

Keeping abreast of product changes and price alterations

The apparently simple task of noting price and product alterations is frequently neglected by all departments of companies. The major problem is caused by the failure to give adequate notice of forthcoming alterations. Price alterations should be scheduled for a specific date, possibly some two months in advance. Once these alterations are notified to the sales force, the wise representative will take the trouble to notify verbally all customers in his or her territory.

Notifying customers is a courtesy which can be turned to excellent use by increasing sales. Most customers do expect annual price increases, product improvements or deletions from the range, and will certainly appreciate forward notice. The wise representative will ensure that the opportunity for 'forward' ordering in advance of the price increase is given to clients.

14.3   Customer service and relations

Assisting customers with their problems

A professional representative is not merely restricted to pushing products to customers, but is concerned to offer a complete service. If customers believe that they will continue to enjoy service after the sale, and have a contact point for any problems which may arise, then the hesitant buyer will be prepared to invest.

Customer problems in commercial selling can usually be traced to other departments of the company. An invoice is incorrect, a delivery is delayed, or dispatch have forwarded an incorrect product. In this case it is the task of the representative to act on behalf of the customer in seeking the cause of the problem and ensuring corrective action is taken. Remember to contact the customer with your results, or the details of progress to date. Do not rely upon the department concerned to carry out your job by contacting the customer. By dealing fairly and quickly with problems, you will build up a store of goodwill in the mind of the client.

Arranging additional services for customers

The responsibility of a representative does not cease at the close of the sale, but continues during the lifetime of the product purchased. The role of after-sales service in customer satisfaction cannot be underestimated. High standards of service will ensure the customer returns to repurchase. The technical skills of the sales engineer are utilised to ensure customers continue to be satisfied with their purchase, often by a follow-on visit following installation.

When involved in lengthy negotiations to secure an order, representatives will often call on the skills of qualified members of the staff to assist in presenting their proposals. In the purchase of major capital equipment, a team of professionals will be involved, to ensure that all aspects of the installation are designed correctly.

Settling customer complaints

When seeking to deal with customer complaints, it is always wise to assume the motivation for complaint is genuine. Present consumer legislation gives considerable protection to the buyer, which, with increasing awareness of these rights, has made the rule of *caveat emptor* ('let the buyer beware') a relic of the past.

Most reputable companies operate a structured complaints system. This ensures that any complaints on product quality are fully investigated by the quality control department, and remedial measures taken if required. The role of the representative is to deal fairly but firmly with the root of the complaint, and seek to correct the situation. A careful note should be taken of the circumstances of the complaint, noting date of purchase, customer name and address, usage, and the definition of the problem. Exchange of product, refund of purchase price, issue of credit note, or discount against a further purchase, are all methods of dealing with a justifiable complaint.

Example

Jim Connor is the senior sales engineer for Quota Sales, involved in negotiating the sale of a large computer system to a multinational company. At each stage Jim can call on the professional skills and specialist knowledge of the:

(a) system designer – to computerise the customer's work system;
(b) electrical engineer – to design and plan the installation;
(c) computer programmer – to tailor the system to suit the client;
(d) training officer – to arrange customer staff training;
(e) accounting technician – to discuss costings, investment, etc.

To present a full and comprehensive brief to the client for such a major system purchase, Jim acts as the leader of a team, ensuring that all aspects of the negotiation are fully researched and planned.

Assisting customers to maintain adequate stock levels

In a marketing context the maintenance of adequate stock levels will exert a direct influence on the amount of sales expected. Whatever marketing efforts are undertaken to move the product into the hands of the final consumer, they will be negated by low or non-existent stock. Let us consider the results of low stocks prior to a sales promotion:

demand for the product is produced by the marketing efforts;

stock proves to be unavailable in the outlets;
customers are frustrated in their wish to purchase;
customers will make the purchase, but choose a competing brand;
competition will in fact benefit from the sales promotion.

Representatives should retain accurate records of the customer's purchase patterns, and should consider offering to physically check stocks to ensure correct levels. Provided the stock check is carried out with accuracy, and no attempt is made by the representative to falsify sales turnover, buyers will appreciate the additional level of service offered. With accurate stock figures the buyer is assured of sufficient stock to meet all sales or production demands.

Establishing effective personal relationships with clients

A fine line exists in the client-representative relationship. At all times the representative should maintain a friendly relationship, based on mutual respect. As a representative of the company, too close a relationship could result in a conflict between the interests of the customer as a friend and the requirements of the company.

Discounts and special terms could be offered to these preferred customers, not merited by the turnover they produced. Customers are also quite likely to refuse a close friend an order, believing they are less likely to be upset, than to refuse a salesperson who maintains a firm but friendly relationship.

Training customer's sales staff, if required

As we have already noted, sales representatives will possess greater product knowledge than customers or customers' sales staff. Representatives will therefore be expected to disseminate this knowledge through organised training sessions. These training sessions enable customers' sales staff to fully understand the features of the product and to improve their selling skills.

The experience of training any group of people in product knowledge is of benefit to the representative. The skills learnt during the training sessions will enable the representative to sell more effectively to large groups of customers. Always remember that selling to a group requires a different style of presentation to that of personal face to face selling. Those attending cannot ask questions of the representatives, nor, by the same rule, can the representative check progress towards closing the sale.

Arranging product information and usage sessions

This area of a representative's duties could well be carried out as a formal session within a client company. The intention is often to ensure that members of a company understand any special operational requirements of a new product.

Example

Stuart Watson has negotiated the sale of photocopiers to an import and export company. The copiers have a number of special features enabling export documents to be produced from a master transparent sheet. Following delivery, Stuart returns to the company and arranges a series of product demonstrations for staff. During these short training sessions he demonstrates the new features, explaining the benefits of the system, and encourages the staff to use the machines under his supervision. By carrying out this particular after-sales service, he ensures the copiers will be used correctly and that staff appreciate the reasons for the purchase being made. Thus the possibility of staff complaints will be reduced. The company management are delighted with the response of their staff to the alteration in working procedures, the system produces the expected savings in time, and they happily consider installing further copiers.

Production usage and demonstration should conform to these simple rules. The representatives should:

explain to the customer which feature will be demonstrated
'I shall be demonstrating the way this photocopier produces enlargements, by means of this simple series of control steps.'

demonstrate the feature in operation
'We set this control button to A5 size . . . insert the paper in this tray . . . press copier function . . . set copy number . . .'

confirm understanding of the feature
'Now I am sure you saw how the machine produced the enlargement using just four simple operations.'

allow customers to use the feature for themselves
'Would you please choose a document you wish to enlarge and practise the operation yourself . . .'

For complicated products where the functions are not readily visible, flip charts, slide sequences or short video programmes should be utilised to ensure the features are clearly understood.

An element of showmanship should be inserted into the demonstration to ensure customers' continued attention. To demonstrate the robustness of a product, sales staff may request the heaviest person present to stand or sit on the product. Test carefully before the demonstration takes place that this type of activity is possible with your product. Any product being demonstrated should be carefully inspected before the event, and if any doubt exists the product should be replaced by a new sample. Customers will quickly notice if the product appears to have been in use for some time. It is wise to ensure that a spare product is carried to the demonstration in case of product failure.

Maintaining special displays and promotions

Special displays and promotions act as a short-term boost to sales. They will require regular attention to ensure that the standard of display does not drop. The impact is considerably reduced if the products on display appear damaged through handling, or require cleaning. Maintenance of the display is the responsibility of the sales representative or merchandiser. Displays should be removed after the period of the promotion is ended.

14.4   Administration

Keeping records of customer information and calls made

Representatives are universally known for their poor administrative skills, despite the importance of sales data to the company. Companies will normally provide control forms to their sales staff, for completion both daily and weekly. They are designed to supply the sales management and marketing departments with the information they need to check sales turnover, and to monitor representative performance in the field. An example of a customer record card and a daily control form are given in Figure 14.2.

Fig. 14.2 *Customer Record Card and Control Form*

CUSTOMER RECORD CARD

NAME QUOTA SALES
COMPANY CONTACT MR. LEWIS
COMPANY TYPE WHOLESALER
CALL DAY THURSDAY

ADDRESS UNIT 7, HILLFIELD ESTATE.
TELEPHONE 779-0274
BANKERS MIDLAND
WEEKLY, MONTHLY, MONTHLY

DATE	CALL	CONTACT	RESULT
4/1	QUOTE FOR CX/500/D	MR LEWIS	PRICE FOR DELIVERY JUNE
6/2	CHASE QUOTATION	MR LEWIS	SENT 10/2

ANNUAL TURNOVER 10,500   PRODUCT RANGE CX/500/CD/500

CALL PATTERN   (J) (F) M A M J J A S O N D

DAILY CONTROL FORM

REPRESENTATIVE CAROLINE WATSON
DATE 4/1   AREA WEST MIDLAND CODE WM/6

CALL	CONTACT	O/E/Q	COMMENT	ACTION
QUOTA SALES	MR LEWIS	QUOTE	CX/500/D 4mm	PASS TO OFFICE
INT. DISTRIBUTORS	MR MYER	ENQUIRY	CLEANING PACK	SAMPLE LEFT
UNV. PRODUCTS	MR YORKE	ORDER	500-CD/600	TO STORES
NADEN ENG	MRS BAKER	ENQUIRY	600 GEAR CLAMP	SEND SAMPLE

VEHICLE FORD ORION
CVD 7901

EXPENSES MEALS 7.50
          FUEL   5.00
          OIL
MILEAGE   START 17071
          FINISH 17138
DAY TOTAL   57

Customer record card

The most vital record a representative can possess, the customer record card forms a documentary summary of customer details, and should always be kept fully up to date. Brief details of company address, telephone and telex numbers and company executives are noted, together with a record of the matters raised during the last client visit. Records can be organised either alphabetically, sequenced in call order or arranged by order of visit.

Duplicates of all record cards should be retained in a safe place, in case of loss. Prospective representatives should be fully aware of the importance of these records. They form the basis of their continued success in selling. When leaving their employment, the records of customers are a valuable record of information to representatives.

Weekly or daily report sheet

Completed reports are forwarded to the area sales manager with details of the calls made during the period. Sales targets are set for the representative to achieve, and the report will show the progress towards achieving these targets. The following sales ratios are produced for the sales manager from the information supplied, to determine the effectiveness of the representative:

- Calls made – orders gained;
  gives an indication of the success of the representative in closing the sale.
- Calls made – orders requested;
  indicates the success of a representative in seizing the opportunity to quote for major orders.
- New calls – existing calls;
  determines the representative's success in gaining new business (cold calls). One of the more difficult areas of selling, and often neglected by the less confident representative.
- Calls – order value;
  illustrates if the representative is undertaking a large number of small calls and neglecting the more demanding large companies.
- Sales turnover – sales turnover target;
  an ongoing comparison giving progress towards achieving the required sales target.

Carrying out routine correspondence

In view of the demands placed on the time available for selling, the quantity of correspondence sent to the representative should be closely monitored. Before information is requested from a representative, both management and marketing should ensure that the information is unobtainable from internal sources.

Copies of correspondence received from customers within a representative area should be forwarded to his or her home address for information and possible comment. The representative should not be required to carry out day-to-day correspondence with the company's customers. This duty is undertaken in larger companies by sales administrators who act as a contact point between customer, company and representative. It is then the duty of the representative to answer promptly all requests sent to him or her.

Often working for long periods away from the environment of a company office, representatives tend to attach a low priority to written correspondence. This situation, if allowed to continue, can cause considerable friction between the home office and the sales force. All new members of a sales team will benefit from a period of familiarisation in the administration department of the company.

Following up enquiries

Through responses to company advertising, or through requests for supplies received from new business ventures, the representative will receive regular listings of enquiries. These prospective clients will require an initial visit to introduce the company range of products, to verify that the customer meets the company criteria, and to complete the formalities of opening a credit account. These calls should be made as speedily as possible to ensure that customer interest is retained, and representatives from competing companies do not seize the initiative.

Obtaining display and merchandising materials

Representatives will carry in their company vehicle a selection of display aids and merchandising materials (if the products merit this). Certain larger display aids, product display stands, specialised promotion items, will often be available from a centralised depot following a written request from the representative. These will be delivered to the specified outlet from the display manufacturer, or through a sub-contracted storage/delivery organisation.

Checking customer credit rating

Company criteria will determine what terms are offered. This will depend on whether the prospective customer is a manufacturer, wholesaler or retailer. Care should be taken to ensure that no goods are supplied on credit before completion of a credit account application. Customers should be informed of the requirement to check on their financial background, and that if goods are urgently required, payment will be on *pro-forma* invoice only. Credit application forms will normally require details of the customer's bankers and two existing suppliers, together with expected annual purchases.

Controlling travel, telephone and other expenses

A major proportion of the expenses incurred by a sales force is consumed by travel. At the end of each calendar month a form is completed by the sales force giving a breakdown of the expenditure. This will cover the receipted purchases of petroleum products, servicing of the vehicle and valeting.

A proportion of the private telephone rental charges, and all business calls, are met by the representative's employer. Telephone charge cards are often supplied for calls made away from home or office. As part of the benefit structure given to representatives, certain amounts may be allowed for meals, use of the home as an office, or subscriptions to organisations of benefit to the company. Expenditure on entertaining of customers is normally met by the company, but care should be taken that the level of entertainment is not excessive.

The offering of gifts or personal favours designed to influence a buyer's decision is a criminal offence, and should neither be attempted or condoned. If such a suggestion is made by a buyer, or any other customer employees, the circumstances should be reported immediately to the representative's area manager for action to be taken.

Payment is normally made after expenses are incurred and the amounts have been checked as correct. On first joining a company, representatives will normally be given a sufficient sum to act as a float for the first month's expenditure. Any representative who foolishly attempts to falsify expenses, by claiming private expenditure as having taken place under a business heading, can expect dismissal.

Communicating items of interest to market intelligence

While in the field, the sales representative is ideally placed to hear information on competitor activity. These items should be communicated by letter to the marketing department. Insignificant items when collated will often give a clear indication of the marketing activities, pricing structures and sales promotion plans of competitors. Without a formal reporting structure, and encouragement to report all items of interest, information vital to the marketing department can be lost. Representatives should be notified of the receipt of their reports, and the conclusions drawn by the marketing department.

The marketing department should ensure the circulation of all market intelligence conclusions to representatives, together with requests for further reports on specified competitors or areas of interest. Even the smallest sales force can provide useful information for management.

Organising the sales area

When first joining a company, the field sales representative will normally be given a complete listing of all existing customers within the specified sales area. Areas will vary in size, dependent upon the number of customers for which the sales representative is responsible. In a sales area covering a major city, the number of calls may well be the same as a rural area, but the mileage travelled will be considerably less. However, if the time taken to travel between calls is taken into account, it may well prove quicker in the rural area.

Correct organisation of the sales area journey is essential if 'face to face' selling-time is to be maximised. The inexperienced representative will busily flit from call to call, with no attempt at planning the day's journey. This inefficiency will result in a high number of 'call backs' caused by clients being unavailable on arrival. Figure 14.3 illustrates the correct breakdown of a sales area into individual journeys for each day.

Fig. 14.3 *Breakdown of Sales Area*

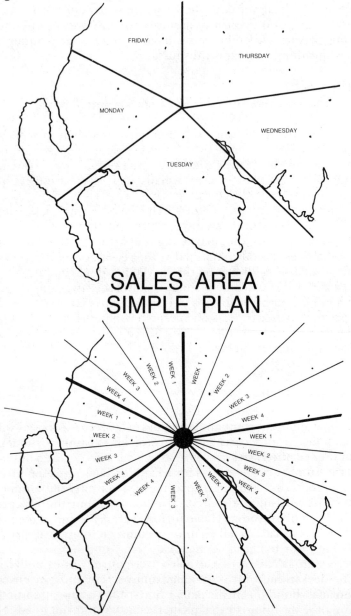

SALES AREA
SIMPLE PLAN

SALES AREA DIVIDED FURTHER
BY WEEKS

All calls in the total sales area are firstly plotted by their location on a suitably scaled map, and subsequently divided into approximately equal sizes. Each sub-area will therefore contain a similar number of calls. The calls undertaken on Monday of each week are completed as far as possible, any call backs being held over to the following day. The calls required on Tuesday are physically adjacent to those undertaken on the previous day, making the task of calling back less demanding in time and mileage. This process is continued throughout the working week, ensuring a regular planned journey is undertaken.

Figure 14.4 illustrates the method of organising the sales area where the calls are separated by longer distances. Travelling is undertaken early in the day, so the representative arrives at the furthest call away from base with the remainder of the day available for calls. This method ensures that as the working day progresses the remaining calls are close to the home base. If calls are made at the commencement of the day, with the intention of travelling further, you can be sure that the clients situated at the end of the journey will never see the representative from one month to the next. Time in hand is the most precious asset a sales representative can possess. Poor area planning wastes time, and loses sales. Correct planning improves efficiency, and improves success.

Arranging call frequencies and pattern

There is a natural tendency on the part of representatives to spend more time with those clients who conduct business in a relaxed and pleasant manner. The social preamble, the welcome invitation to coffee, and the easy-to-obtain order can divert a representative from the more formal and difficult client.

To counter this very human tendency, the representative must carefully allocate selling-time to each client based purely on sales turnover, and not upon their friendship or liking for a particular customer. Let us calculate the time available to a representative for selling, prior to constructing a call frequency chart.

The average sales representative will be available for selling on only 235 days in each year, allowing for a five-day working week and normal holiday entitlement. If we assume an average working day, we discover that the total selling-time available is around 1880 hours each year. Dividing our number of clients into the hours available for calling may show each client is entitled to a total annual allocation of time of five hours.

Fig. 14.4 *Long Distance Sales Journey Plan*

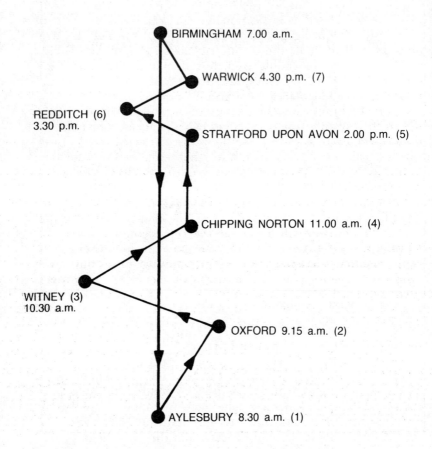

If we consider the call frequency pattern further, we realise that some customers will require longer than five hours' selling-time in a year, while others will require considerably less. We must therefore classify our calls by sales turnover, and allocate time for calling in accordance with this figure.

Example

Stephen Bond is responsible for the Midlands sales area of his company, selling a range of giftware to retailers, whole-salers and mail order discount houses. He has a list of 400 customers requiring sales calls. He grades his calls by their annual sales turnover, and discovers the following breakdown of sales:

(a) 80 Large customers   – annual turnover £10 000 +
(b) 200 Medium customers – annual turnover £4000 +
(c) 120 Small customers   – annual turnover £1000

He decides that large customers should be visited at least fortnightly in order to ensure the correct level of service. Medium customers should be visited at least monthly, and small customers need only be seen every six months. He calculates the number of calls he is required to make each year as:

(a) Large customers   - 8 calls per day
(b) Medium customers   - 2 calls per day
(c) Small customers   - 1 call per day

A total call rate, each day, of 11 sales visits will give Stephen time to seek new customers for his products. He will also be able to spend time with his medium-sized customers, increasing the size of their orders, or introducing new products to them. Having broken his sales calls into categories, considered the number of calls each needs, and calculated his daily call rates, Stephen is now confident that his sales targets can be achieved.

14.5 Summary

In this chapter we have considered the organisation of the sales force, and the characteristics and duties of a professional representative. Selling brings high rewards, in salary and benefits, together with a high sense of personal achievement. Career development would be by progression into sales management, and later into marketing.

The skills gained from experience in the field prove beneficial in communication and motivation within marketing. As practical discipline, qualifications are of less importance than ability and experience. Representatives seeking career moves should consider undertaking a training course in sales management at their local college of further education, or joining as a student member the Institute of Marketing Diploma Course in Sales Management.

Assignment 1

You are a sales assistant in a retail electrical store, and are approached by Mr and Mrs Hastings, who are seeking a birthday gift for their teenage son. They consider that a portable stereo record player would be an attractive choice. Using a model with which you are familiar, describe the benefits which you consider would assist Mr and Mrs Hastings in their choice. Detail three possible objections they may well raise, and the answers you would give.

Assignment 2

Video closed circuit television equipment is used extensively in all types of sales training. While appearing in front of a camera places a certain amount of strain on the participants, this pressure provides a situation close to real life. Remember it is considerably easier to make initial errors in a practice situation and have them corrected, than to make those same errors in the field, and lose a customer as a consequence.

The following scenario is designed to enable students to practise the full range of selling skills. The video recording should be scheduled for a maximum of 15 minutes. Upon completion the video should be replayed and assessed using the checklist supplied in Figure 14.5.

Representative's brief

You are the new area sales representative for Universal Products, and you are calling for the first time, by appointment, on the buyer for International Distributors. From the sales records kept by the previous representative, you know that the company has not ordered from your range for the past four months, despite previous high sales turnover. You also understand that an ex-representative of your company has recently started in business manufacturing a similar range of products to yours. Other

Fig. 14.5 *Sales Presentation Evaluation Form*

Name of Salesperson
Product

1. *Initial approach*   YES/NO
   (a) Introduced self, company, product.
   (b) Introduction appropriate.
   (c) Had a pleasant, friendly manner.
   (d) Discovered prospect's need or problem.
   (e) Had a good opening statement.

2. *Presentation*
   (a) Asked questions to determine needs.
   (b) Demonstrated benefits of product.
   (c) Let customer participate.
   (d) Endeavoured to gain commitment from customer.
   (e) Well-organised sales presentation.
   (f) Answered objections satisfactorily.
   (g) What objections were raised by customer?
       1 . . .
       2 . . .
       3 . . .

3. *Closing the sale*
   (a) Did salesperson help customer decide?
   (b) What buying signals were given by customer?
       1 . . .
       2 . . .
       3 . . .
   (c) Did salesperson make any trial closes?
   (d) What type of closes were attempted?
       1 . . .
       2 . . .
       3 . . .

4. *Increasing the sale*
   (a) Suggested additional purchase.
       1 Related item
       2 Larger size
       3 Multiple purchase
       4 Special sale product
   (b) Made positive suggestion.
   (c) Showed or demonstrated suggested product.
   (d) Stressed advantage of buying merchandise.

5. *General comments*
   (a) Did salesperson control the sale?
   (b) Did salesperson seem confident of making the sale?
   (c) Was salesperson courteous and helpful?
   (d) Was salesperson sold on own product?
   (e) Did salesperson display empathy with customer?

customers have been given prices that match any prices you may be offering.

Your task is to see the buyer of International Distributors and introduce the product you have chosen from the wide Universal Products range. You are seeking an order for this product, which is shortly to be advertised extensively. International Distributors are the largest wholesalers of products within your sales area, and it is essential to your company marketing policy that they undertake to stock your product.

Buyer's brief

The new representative for Universal Products has made an appointment with you at 9.00 am on Tuesday. You have dealt with them for some five years and consider them a reliable, if slightly old-fashioned company. You understand that the previous representative has now left Universal and started in business manufacturing a similar range of items. However, no-one from Universal has been to see you for about three months. As the buyer for International Distributors, you are seeking a new range of products to offer customers. As always, price is a big factor in your decision, but delivery and quality are of equal importance. You look forward to seeing the new representative, but wish to discover why you have not been visited for the last three months.

Index